CENTER
STAGE

CENTER STAGE

A demystifying account of the events of
Nebuchadnezzar's
dream of Daniel 2.

NORMA P. GILLETT

authorHOUSE®

AuthorHouse™ LLC
1663 Liberty Drive
Bloomington, IN 47403
www.authorhouse.com
Phone: 1-800-839-8640

Scripture taken from the Holy Bible, NEW INTERNATIONAL VERSION®. Copyright © 1973, 1978, 1984, 2011 by Biblica, Inc. All rights reserved worldwide. Used by permission.

NEW INTERNATIONAL VERSION® and NIV® are registered trademarks of Biblica, Inc. Use of either trademark for the offering of goods or services requires the prior written consent of Biblica US, Inc.

Published by AuthorHouse   06/03/2014

ISBN: 978-1-4772-9273-0 (sc)
ISBN: 978-1-4772-9239-6 (hc)
ISBN: 978-1-4772-9272-3 (e)

Library of Congress Control Number: 2012922189

Any people depicted in stock imagery provided by Thinkstock are models, and such images are being used for illustrative purposes only.
Certain stock imagery © Thinkstock.

This book is printed on acid-free paper.

DEDICATION

Dedicated to my family and close friends
who encouraged me and prayed for me.
May the Holy Spirit kindle a flame of living fire in your hearts.

Acknowledgement

Thank God from whom all blessings flow. I humbly thank Him for all His benefits. To all those who have helped in anyway, my children, Sean Calliard, Lawford & Isabelle Campbell, Jonel Clarke, Roy & Delveen Ebanks, Angella Fairweather, Talice Foster, Devon Hines, Kevoun Morgan, Pastors: Astor Bowers, Roy Gordon and Noel Rose, thank you.

CONTENTS

PREFACE

Unto 2300 Days

In years past, I found the 2300 Days Prophecy very challenging and hard to understand. It was not until I prayed earnestly to God for wisdom and understanding that the meaning came very clear to me. After that revelation, I explained it to my church under the guidance of the Holy Spirit.

One day as I was reviewing the sequence of events, the Holy Spirit said, I should write it. A few days after, He prompted me to write it. I decided to write the information along with illustrations and pass it on to the members of the church. I got a little comfortable with that idea, but the Spirit impressed me to print so others who have difficulties as I had could benefit. For some time I told myself, it was not practical to write my first book on such a challenging topic. The more I tried to reason the idea away, the stronger became the conviction.

Finally, I started and worked on the script conscientiously, which took me close to a year. The whole concept was much bigger than I anticipated and later that year I decided to conclude, but I needed to do some outside research to culminate the writing. That was when the unbelievable happened. The script went missing. I searched everywhere, still no success. I felt very dejected, and disappointed to know all the hard work was for nothing.

After many failed searches, I accepted the reality and counted my loss. After some time the Spirit impressed me to do what I feared all along. "Start over." "What?" It was impossible to remember all I wrote, this was not happening. At that point, in the whole experience, I felt woefully inadequate to think there was even a remote possibility to start, let alone finish. Months passed, then one night as I lay awake in bed, I talked to God and He assured me, He would be with me. The next morning, I started in earnest. God be praised.

INTRODUCTION

Jesus warned His disciples about some who would enter the flock appearing as sheep, but would be wolves in sheep clothing. Not everyone who comes in the name of Jesus is genuine. He wants everyone to know Him personally, so detecting the genuine would not be a problem.

Center Stage seeks to arouse attention to the dream of Nebuchadnezzar king of Babylon in Daniel 2. "What significance is this to us in our day?" The answer is more than we can imagine.

This dream symbolized kings and kingdoms from the time of Nebuchadnezzar to the end of the world, when God will set up His eternal kingdom. There were four major kingdoms represented by metals, ranging from the most precious to the least in value.

Though God honored Nebuchadnezzar by making him the head of gold, he wanted to be more than head, he wanted his kingdom to last forever, so he made an image of gold in defiance of God's will. Similar kingdoms after him have been defiant and have even introduced counterfeit worship in place of giving homage to God. They usurp the worship and the title due to God and many worshippers follow blindly because of ignorance.

The writer through much prayer and research has sought to bring to the surface many actions past and present, that are counterfeit and contrary to the commands of God. There is conflict between good and evil. These two opposing powers are vying for recognition in worship and for "Center Stage." The events as they unfold throughout history signify that the battle is waging, there is a controversy between the commands of God and the traditions of man. Sometimes it would seem as if evil is winning, but good will ultimately triumph because God is in charge.

The blatant defiance of the truth seems to have everyone's attention. It would seem evil has taken center stage but God will have the last word, His will and way will last forever. Kings and kingdoms will soon pass away, but the Stone cut out of the mountain without hands will ultimately destroy the image and will fill the earth; God will set up His everlasting kingdom. That is "Good News."

CHAPTER 1

Daniel a Captive in Babylon

Daniel authored his book in the 6th century. The theme of this prophetic book is, "God is in Control." Daniel was among the Hebrew captives taken to Babylon by king Nebuchadnezzar, when he overthrew Jerusalem.

> The prophecies of Daniel thus provide a divinely constructed bridge from the precipice of time to the boundless shores of eternity a bridge over which those who, like Daniel, purpose in their hearts, to serve God.[1]

> The historical section of the book of Daniel reveals, in the most striking manner, the true philosophy of history. This section stands as a preface to the prophetic section. By providing a detailed account of God's dealings with one nation, Babylon, the book enables us to understand the meaning of the rise and fall of other nations out lined in the portion of the book. [2]

The philosophical and historical component of the book of Daniel make it easy to understand the story, as it relates to the meaning of the rise and fall of other nations as revealed in the book. Without this clear understanding, the role of Babylon and succeeding nations in the divine plan, cannot be fully understood or appreciated.

History shows Daniel facing the wise heathen king Nebuchadnezzar, monarch of the most powerful nation of the time. In *Jeremiah* 27:6, God called Nebuchadnezzar His servant. He also called other heathen rulers to perform His will; among whom were the Persian kings Darius and Cyrus. (More detailed account in later chapters.) Little did Daniel know that he had a part to play in God's divine plan. He was to play that pivotal role in securing the submission of the king's will to the will of God, to make the divine will of God possible.

God needed a loyal one in the court of Babylon who would be a true representative of the principles and policies of heaven. Daniel was the man. The circumstances that brought about Daniel a Hebrew captive, to the favorable attention of the king of Babylon, was providential. Furthermore, the fact that the king came to acknowledge Daniel first and then his God, indicates God's plan to use humans in accomplishing His work on earth through human agents.

God could use Daniel because he was a man of impeccable character, a man whose primary business was to honor God. *Daniel* 1:8 says "Daniel purposed in his heart" . . . and God allowed him to find favor in the eyes of the officials of Babylon. This decision on Daniel's part paved the way for the demonstration of physical and intellectual superiority. God gave him and his friends wisdom, skill and knowledge in all learning. These attributes made them "ten times better" than their rivals in personality, physique and intellect, and thereby won the respect and confidence of Nebuchadnezzar.

The succeeding events of chapters 2, 3 and 4, brought Nebuchadnezzar to acknowledge the inferiority of humans. He declared, "Of a truth it is that your God is a God of gods, and a Lord of kings, and a revealer of secrets." When brought before the king as one who could interpret dreams, Daniel acknowledged God as the revealer of secrets.

Do not miss opportunities to witness for the hope in Jesus, give Him the praise and acknowledgements for battles fought and victories won. Let God be praised and honored, not self. What has Daniel experience taught? Even in times of greatest trials, remember who is in charge.

Daniel's faithfulness to God landed him in a den of hungry lions. How did he get there when the king himself admitted Daniel had an excellent spirit in him and made him chief of the officers? Daniel, a foreigner, was now chief officer. What great honor, but this promotion also made Daniel a target for his rivals. These jealous officers decided to get rid of him permanently by setting a trap requiring him to cease his daily prayer routine. They knew he would not stop praying regardless of outside resistance.

The unsuspecting king honored the request these caviling men asked of him. This was what they needed. Daniel was finished, or so they thought. The thought of hungry lions did not intimidate Daniel even for a day, because he trusted in God. He showed his trust in God by praying the way he usually did.

The world today would do well with more men with character like that of Daniel. One famous writer says, "God is looking for men who are true to principle, as the needle to the pole." God is looking for loyal children who will give Him "Center Stage" in their lives. Do not think for one moment that it was easier to be loyal then, than it is now. Those were dangerous days. Think of someone caging lions, starving them and feeding them humans as lunch.

Furthermore, there was little or no consequence for the perpetrators. The laws of the Medes and Persians were unchangeable. Those with evil intentions could easily have their way, if they obtained the king's seal of approval. This was Daniel's experience and the jealous men who wanted him dead.

His enemies were both dumb founded and happy to see him publicly praying to God, as he usually did, so they hurried to the king to report the matter. The king was sick with fear, for it was only then he realized what these men really wanted to do to Daniel. He tried hard to deliver him, but these scheming men reminded him that the law of the Medes and Persians are unchangeable. When the efforts of earthly kings fail, a King in heaven never fails, so the king assures Daniel that, "Thy God . . . He will deliver thee"(*Daniel* 6:16)

Daniel was able to do what he did because he had a heart connection with God. He purposed in his heart, so we too need this "heart" connection with God. History is replete with incidents where God's children were: persecuted, beaten, burnt at the stake, hanged, tortured and shot for their belief in God. It happened in Daniel's day, in the dark days, in the days of Luther and Huss and it is going to happen again. How will it fear with you dear reader? Will you be faithful like Daniel? May God help you to have a heart relationship with Him.

[1]   Fernon Retzer & Mike Speegle (*You Can Understand The Bible*) p.15.

[2]   S.D.A. Bible Commentary Vol., 4, p.750.

CHAPTER 2

Abraham to his Third Generation

God had made a promise to faithful Abraham to give him a son of promise, through whom all the families of the earth would be blessed. Isaac was born when Abraham and his wife were old and he lived with his parents until manhood. Though they loved him very much it was now time for him to establish a family of his own. Abraham charged his faithful servant with the responsibility of finding a wife for his beloved son, Isaac. This he did and God led him to Rebekah, the daughter of Laban and Bethuel.

Isaac and Rebekah had twin sons named Esau and Jacob. Isaac's favorite son was Esau the hunter, and the favorite of Rebekah was Jacob, the one who stayed close home. Jacob stole Esau's birthright, then his blessing. These actions caused tension in the family because Esau displayed anger towards Jacob. His mother feared for his safety, so she sent him to his uncle Laban in Padanaram.

God blessed Jacob and made him a promise that He would bring him back home. Jacob spent many years with his uncle and served him faithfully. He also had done well for himself and was now rich. It was now time to return home with his two wives and children, and all the wealth he had acquired in Padanaram.

Though twenty years was a long time, it was not long enough for him to forget what he had done to his brother. The thought of facing his brother gave him great trepidation to return home. He tried to appease his brother by offering him gifts, and calling him lord. The night before he faced his brother, he sent everyone over the brook Jabbok, and he was alone on that side of the brook praying for God's guidance and intervention. God had a surprise for him that night before he crossed the water into Esau's territory.

God appeared to him and he thought an enemy was trying to hurt him, so he fought all night long, until almost daybreak. The angel told him to let him go for it was nearly daybreak. Jacob then realized it was not a man, so he told Him he would not, unless He blessed him. The angel blessed him and changed his name from Jacob to Israel (*Genesis* 27-32).

Jacob (now Israel), had twelve sons, favorite of whom was Joseph. To show his love for him, Jacob made him a beautiful coat of many colors. The brothers were not happy at all. Their relationship with him was not great, and to worsen the situation, Joseph had two dreams that indicated his brothers would some day bow down to him. They determined that, that would not happen.

As time passed, their opportunity came, when one day their father sent Joseph with food to the brothers who were tending animals far from home. They described him as the dreamer, and wanted to kill him, but the eldest brother Reuben said no, put him in a pit. (He wanted to save him). They put him in the pit, but before long they saw some Ishmeelites on their way to Egypt. Judah the fourth of the brothers suggested that they sell him. This they did for twenty pieces of silver, which they divided among them.

To Reuben's surprise, when he returned to the pit, Joseph was gone. Reuben was very upset and tore his clothes. The brothers dipped Joseph's coat in the blood of a kid and sent it to their father saying they found it. Jacob thinking Joseph met a terrible fate tore his clothes and mourned for his son for a long time.

Meanwhile, the merchants took him to Egypt and sold him to Potiphar, captain of the king's guard. God was with Joseph and he prospered and found favor with Potiphar, who made him overseer in his house and everything he had. God blessed his master's house because of him.

Joseph was in a strange land, among strange people and customs. It would be easy to adopt these new behaviors but he did not, he remained faithful to God and God blessed him. Maybe it is time to say a prayer for young people of our day that are keeping their focus and not falling prey to peer pressure and drugs. Parents train your children to fear God out of love, and continue to pray for them.

One day Joseph's reputation came crashing down, when his mistress Potiphar's wife wanted to have a relationship with him. He said no, and she grabbed him. He ran leaving his coat in her hand. She used the garment to lie to her workers, and her husband, who threw him into jail. Joseph continued to be faithful in jail and was a source of help and encouragement to fellow inmates. The jailer acknowledged his demeanor and gave him charge over the other inmates.

It is wonderful to know God is always with His children in every circumstance. No circumstance should be too rigorous and unforgiving that should cause unfaithfulness to God. Peter, Paul and Silas were beaten and threatened but they had no fear for their lives. Martin Luther, Huss and Jerome were threatened but they remained faithful. Martin Luther King Jr., stood up for justice for he had a dream.

After years in jail, the king recalled Joseph to the palace and made him governor of Egypt, second in line to the Pharoah. Part of his responsibility was to have enough food in store for seven years of famine. All the plans he put in place during the seven years of plenty, prospered and Pharaoh was pleased.

As the years of famine continued people from all countries including Canaan, came to Egypt to buy food. Joseph's brothers came too. Joseph recognized them immediately, but they did not have a clue that he was Joseph. He spoke to them through an interpreter, and found out the welfare of his youngest brother and their father.

Joseph subjected them to many tests to see if they had changed their old selfish ways. He called them spies, put them all in jail for three days and kept Simeon in jail, and ordered them to bring their little brother, or Simeon would remain in jail. He ordered their money replaced in their sacs, on their return journey.

When Benjamin came on their second trip, Joseph advised his servants to place more food on Benjamin's plate, during dinner with them. Joseph observed their behavior with Benjamin's special treatment, but not one of them complained. For their return journey, he ordered everyone's money placed in their sacs, and his favorite cup placed in Benjamin's sac.

Joseph sent pursuers after them to recover according to him his stolen cup. The one that had the cup would die, he said. The brothers were beside themselves to learn Benjamin's sac had the cup. They all returned to Egypt, and for the forth time bowed to Joseph, not having a clue that they were fulfilling his dreams of long ago. True to his words to his father that he would give, his life for Benjamin's, and bring him back; Judah stepped forward to bear the punishment for his brother. He wanted to spare his aged father the agony of living without the son of his old age, seeing Joseph his brother had already died.

For the second time, Joseph was overcome with tears of joy. This time he sent his servants out, and revealed his identity to his brothers. He gave them many gifts and Pharaoh sent wagons for the family to come to Egypt. God told Jacob to go and he would one day bring them back out of the land of Egypt. *This occasion brought Israel to Egypt.*

<u>*Israel in Egypt*</u>

It was a joyful journey to Egypt for Jacob and his family. He and all he had journeyed from Canaan to Egypt. Not only was he anticipating reuniting with Joseph, but also the thought of returning to his homeland some day, encouraged him. God made him a promise.

"I will go down to Egypt with you, and bring you back home again, and you will see your son Joseph and he will be there to close your eyes when you die" (*Genesis* 46: 4 CW).

Joseph and Pharaoh welcomed Jacob and his family and gave them the land of Goshen as their home. Everything was pleasant for them and their animals and Jacob lived seventeen years in Egypt. Before Jacob died, he blessed his children and grand children, and repeated to Joseph the promise God had made to him to take him back to his homeland. His request to Joseph was that he should take his bones back home.

All Egypt mourned for Jacob when he died, and after forty days of mourning all Pharaoh's servants, Joseph and his brethren, the elders of his house and all the elders of Egypt went to Canaan to bury Jacob. Upon their return to Egypt, his brothers felt that, now that their father was dead Joseph would take revenge on them for what they had done to him many years ago. Joseph assured them that he would not hurt them, for what they had meant for evil, God meant it for good. Joseph lived happily with his brethren and took good care of them. He saw his children and grand children. Like his father, he charged his brethren to take his bones back to Canaan.

After the death of Joseph, a new Pharaoh who did not know Joseph became ruler. This Pharaoh saw the Israelites as a threat, because he claimed they were many and stronger than were the Egyptians. Out of fear, he contrived a plan to keep their population under control. He set taskmasters over them to distress them with burdens including building cities. These taskmasters made their lives miserable and burdensome. The people made mortar and brick, and worked in the fields.

The king also told the midwives to kill all Hebrew baby boys, and save the girls. However, these Godly women saved the baby boys at birth. Their response to the king when questioned why they did not follow his instructions to destroy the male babies as he commanded, was the babies would be born before they get to the mothers. The king's plan did not succeed, therefore he commanded the people to throw every son that is born into the river.

Recently, (the time this book was written) the news reported the parents of a supposedly dead newborn visited the hospital morgue to take a last look at him. Surprise, relief, joy, a multiplicity of mixed emotions enraptured the dumb-founded parents, when they realized he was alive. Call it a miracle, or whatever you will, but this is nothing short of divine intervention.

Suffice it to say, there is nothing hard for God. He always has the last word. Though the Pharaoh tried to destroy the male babies, God intervened in the preservation of one of these babies.

CHAPTER 3

Moses Born to "Free"

Just about that same time the command was given to destroy the male babies, a couple from the tribe of Levi had a son and decided to hide him. This they did for three months, but time came when they could not keep him any longer. Consequently, the mother hid the baby in a basket and placed it among rushes on the river. His sister Miriam stayed at a safe distance and watched.

The crying baby caught the attention of the Pharaoh's daughter, and she sent her maid to fetch the child. On opening the basket, she knew he belonged to a Hebrew woman, but decided to keep him anyway. Miriam was quick to offer to find a nurse for the baby, to which the princess agreed. The child's mother received pay to take care of her own child. This had to be divine intervention.

"The mother's earnest prayer had committed her child to the care of God; and angel's unseen, hovered above his lowly resting place. Angels directed Pharaoh's daughter thither" (*Patriarchs & Prophets* p.218).

The key component in this incredible rescue story is the prayer of the mother. One writer says this about prayer:

There is necessity for diligence in prayer; let nothing hinder you. Make every effort to keep open the communion between Jesus and your own soul . . . Nothing that in any way concerns our peace is too small for Him to notice. There is no chapter in our experience too dark for Him to read, there is no perplexity too difficult for Him to unravel. No calamity can befall the least of His children, no anxiety harass the soul, no joy cheer, no sincere prayer escapes the lips, of which our heavenly Father is unobservant, or in which He takes no immediate interest. [3]

The faith of these parents is a lesson in time to parents to commit their concerns about their children to God. There is no difficulty too hard that God cannot solve. He will come through for you as He did for them. The Psalmist says, "Commit your way to the Lord; trust in Him and He will watch over you" (*Psalm* 37:5).

It was now the mother's opportunity to use the time with her precious child to train him for God. She had no doubt that this child was born for greatness. She knew with his royal mother; he would encounter teachings, practices and habits that would contradict her principles. Hence, she exercised great care in training him, impressing upon his mind the folly of idol worship, and the benefits of serving the God of heaven and earth.

At twelve years of age the mother took the child to the palace. The Pharaoh's daughter named him Moses, meaning she drew him from the water. During his years in the palace, he received the highest military and civil training possible and was among the favorite leaders of the armies of Egypt. He was of an impeccable character, learned in the wisdom of Egypt, and very intelligent. The king was pleased, and determined to make him his successor.

Despite all these outstanding qualities, and recognition, Moses identified himself with his people the Hebrews or Israelites. He felt sorry for their suffering and pain and the injustice and oppression they felt. He wished he could defend them. One day he noticed an Egyptian abusing a Hebrew worker and he killed aggressor and buried him in the sand.

The next day he tried to encourage two Israelites to settle their misunderstanding, but the offender retorted in a negative way and made mention of the incident of the day before. Word quickly circulated among the Egyptians, who told Pharaoh, that Moses was trying to lead his people against the Egyptians. They went on to say he was trying to overthrow the government and make himself ruler. Pharaoh immediately ordered his execution.

The forty year-old general of Egypt had no choice but to escape for his life. Estranged from the love of his foster mother, loss of the respect and admiration of his adoptive grandfather the Pharaoh of Egypt, the fine furnishings and elegant architecture, Moses was now to enter the school of humility and nature. God in His mercy provided a home for him with Jethro the priest and king of Median.

His new occupation as a shepherd provided him with various opportunities to learn patience, selflessness, compassion, longsuffering and tender solicitude for his flock. Moses spent much time in prayer and meditation. Little did he know that this was preparation for the great work ahead of him. Moses applied himself and his acumen was because of severe mental and moral discipline. Moses became reverent, patient, humble, and "very meek above all men who were upon the face of the earth" (*Numbers 12:3*).

Not only did Moses receive a home and employment from Jethro, but he also married one of his daughters. Year after year as Moses followed his flock from place to place, he thought of his brethren in Egypt. He recounted the promises that were the legacy of the chosen nation. Day by day, his prayers ascended to God on their behalf. The hours he spent in nature away from human influences were beneficial not only to him but to the world that would benefit from his writings, inspired by the Holy Spirit. These books include the book of beginnings, *Genesis* and *The Exodus* among others. Angels surrounded him with light.

In the mean time, the Pharaoh of Egypt died and another took his place. Israel cried to God because of their bondage, and God heard them. He remembered the promise He made to their grandfather and father and to Jacob himself when he went to Egypt. The time for Israel's emancipation had come.

The Burning Bush

One day as Moses led his flock near Horeb, "*The Mountain of God*," he saw a bush; branches, leaves and trunk in flames, but the flames did not affect the bush. His curiosity led him to want to have a close-up view. As he came near, he heard a voice calling his name, telling him to remove his shoes for he was standing on holy ground. God identified himself as the God of Abraham, Isaac and Jacob.

Moses hid his face and God told him He had heard the cry of Israel and had seen their affliction and the ill-treatment by their taskmasters. Moses was terrified when God told him, he was to be the deliverer of Israel from Egyptian bondage. Moses tried hard to excuse himself from the task by claiming ignorance, inadequacy, and did not know whom he should tell them sent them.

God would eliminate all difficulties and give him success. He provided a solution for all these early excuses of Moses. These excuses were because of his diffidence, but God promised him He would put words in his mouth and send Aaron his brother to be his mouthpiece and he was to say, "I AM THAT I AM," sent him.

God told Moses to expect resistance from Pharaoh, but he should be courageous. God was about to perform mighty miracles at the hand of Moses and Aaron that would cause terror to the oppressors of His people, and cause them to want Israel to go. The abuse Israel experienced was about to come to a very dramatic end.

Plagues of Egypt

Armed with the charge God had given to them, Moses and Aaron journeyed to Egypt. Before they even came before the king, word got to him, about the mission of these men to free the Hebrews. He was not a little annoyed. When the men approached him and told him the message from God, he angrily retorted, "Who is Jehovah that I should obey His voice to let Israel go?" "I know not Jehovah, neither will I let Israel go" (*Exodus 5:2*).

He claimed Moses and Aaron were causing the people to be idle, and to aggravate the situation, by asking that they get time to go and offer sacrifice in the wilderness to God. The people were accustomed to receiving straw to make bricks, but now, because of Moses' intervention, things were about to change.

Pharaoh angrily ordered that the people should find their own straw, and make the same amount of bricks as they usually did. The people begged the supervisors to provide straw so they would do a fair day's work, but they received harsh punishment instead. Moses tried to reason with the people but they were angry with him, saying he caused them extra hardship.

Moses did all God told him to do before Pharaoh, to convince him to obey, but he used his magicians to counter the first two plagues. God told Moses to use the rod in his hand to smite the dust and there was lice on man and beast. The magicians could not copy, this they say was "the finger of God." God plagued Egypt at the hand of Moses to urge Pharaoh to let Israel go, but nine out of ten plagues, saw him get harder and harder.

Ten Plagues

- First Plague: **Blood**—in all waters, streams, rivers, ponds, pools.
- Second Plague: **Frogs**—everywhere, house, bedrooms, in beds, house of servants, ovens, kneading troughs.
- Third Plague: **Lice**—in man and beast

- Fourth Plague: **Swarms of flies**—into all the houses, and land of Egypt.
- Fifth Plague: **Murrain**—on all animals of Egypt.
- Sixth Plague: **Boil**—upon man, and beast.
- Seventh Plague: **Hail**—upon man, beast and plants.
- Eighth Plague: **Locusts**—fill the houses and devour plants.
- Ninth Plague: **Darkness**—very thick darkness for three days.
- Tenth Plague: **Death**—of the first born of human and animals.

On the night before the tenth plague occurred. Moses instructed the Israelites to borrow from the Egyptians, jewels of gold and silver, also clothing. They were to kill a kid and daub the blood on their doorposts. They were to roast the flesh and eat it with unleavened bread and bitter herb. They should eat in hast standing, with their waist girded, shoes on and stick in hand. Everyone was to be inside at midnight.

At midnight, the death angel went through Egypt, and every first born of animals and human alike including Pharaoh's son were dead. The death angel passed over the houses that had the blood on the doorposts. Mourning came from all the other homes of the Egyptians. This was too much for Pharaoh he had, had enough and he sent a messenger in haste for Moses and Aaron. He told them to take the people, along with their belongings and go. Pharaoh also asked Moses and Aaron to bless him.

The Egyptians were now glad to let Israel go. They urged them on, fearing if they stayed longer; they might be in danger of something worst happening. The Israelites took everything, even their kneadingtrough and dough, and all the items they had borrowed. They left Egypt on foot about six hundred thousand, Including mixed multitude.

---

[3] Steps to Christ pp. 68, 70.

CHAPTER 4

Disobedience led to Captivity

All the years of their journey through the wilderness Israel constantly murmured, disobeyed and even went as far as to worship idols. It was because of their disobedience and complaining that all except Caleb and Joshua of that original group who left Egypt died in the wilderness. The new generation did little to change that behavior, they continued their apostasy and time and again God forgave them, but ever so often they would break their promise and fall right back into rebellion.

From time to time God would allow other nations to attack or capture them so they would learn and repent, but their repentance was always short lived. In process of time they would be back at their old game. It is only unfortunate that the innocent ones sometimes shared part of the punishment with the guilty.

Jeremiah the prophet predicted one such of their captivities and the overthrow of Jerusalem. This took place in **606 B.C.** during the reign of Jehoiakim king of Judah. Nebuchadnezzar's expedition began near the close of the third year of Jehoiakim's reign. (*Daniel* reckons from this point) However, he did not accomplish subjugation of Jerusalem until nine months into the following year. (*Jeremiah* reckons from this point). Jehoakim humbled himself and spared himself this arduous journey to Babylon. Nebuchadnezzar allowed him to remain in Jerusalem as ruler chargeable to the king of Babylon (*Daniel and The Revelation p.13*). Jeremiah relates the reason Israel became captives of Babylon:

> [8] Because you didn't listen to the Lord, this is what He says [9] I will send for the armies to the north, and my servant Nebuchadnezzar, king of Babylon will come against Judah and her neighbors and will devastate their land leaving their cities in ruins as objects of horror. [10] I will silence the shouts of joy and gladness, the happy voices of the bride and bridegroom, the sound of millstones grinding out rich, wheat, and I will put out the light of late-burning lamps. [11] Judah and her neighbors will be devastated and will come under the control of the king of Babylon seventy years (*Jeremiah* 25: 8-11 CW).

It is interesting to note how the prophecy on the fate of Israel written more than one hundred years before it happened, occurred at the time specified. Isaiah the prophet had told King Hezekiah that all the good things would be carried to Babylon, even his own children, and his descendants would be taken and become eunuchs in the palace of the king (*2 Kings: 20: 14-18*).

The year **606 B.C.**, was the first time Nebuchadnezzar besieged Jerusalem in the first year of his reign. The second time was during the reign of Jehoiachin, son of Jehoiakim king of Judah, Nebuchadnezzar besieged Jerusalem and took the king, his family and the people, including Daniel and many other young men, (but left the poor of the land). All the moveable items from inside and outside the temple were carried to Babylon.

Hebrew Captives in Babylon

During those terrible days, Daniel and his friends found favor in the palace of the king. Though in a strange land they were more respected than they would hope to be in their own land. They accepted what was to be their new life and behaved wisely . . . Little wonder the king showed them kindness and liberality. The people of God should take note of these men. They were in a strange heathen land against their will. They had every reason to murmur and complain, but they did not, they honored God in that strange land. So can you, you do not have to adopt Babylon's principles and customs. God never changes and He will help the striving, even weak ones to overcome.

He helped Joseph in the land of Egypt. Amid wide-spread heathenism and idol worship, Joseph stood for principle. When faced with the choice to succumb to the allurement of Potiphar's wife, he boldly said, "How can I do this great wickedness, and sin against God?" For this, he went to prison. He still did not complain or wallow in self-pity. He remained faithful and the jailer promoted him as he was by Potiphar.

He continued to bless others right there in jail. You too can be a blessing to others wherever you are. You do not have to compromise principles for anyone or anything. Be faithful even if it means death. It is better to lose your life here and find it in God. (Read the story in *Genesis* 39). Samuel stood for principle, and God honored him, even though Eli's sons were living reckless lives right before his eyes.

Why God allowed His People to be Persecuted

God allows people the freedom to choose their course of actions, but sometimes when they abuse this freedom and use it to self-destruct, He gets their attention in some way. Israel repeatedly rebelled and turned their backs on God. Many years before the siege, He sent His prophets to warn them of the consequences of disobedience and rebellion, but those warnings did not deter them. They now had to suffer the embarrassment and loss to Nebuchadnezzar a heathen king. All through the period before the coming of the Messiah, and after His ascension to present, the church is subject to persecution *(Daniel and the Revelation p.34. paraphrased).*

CHAPTER 5

God has a Witness

The early church in **A.D. 325** started out with just a few Jews who followed Christ, but grew rapidly. On the day of Pentecost the number of Jews converted and added to the church in one day was 3000. We also learn in Acts 10 that a Gentile Roman Centurion named Cornelius and his family accepted Christianity. The church grew, but so did persecution against her.

Persecution of the church

For about two and half centuries the cause of persecution of the early church varied. One reason was the refusal to worship the Emperor of Rome, chief of whom was Nero. This refusal was punishable by death, and many of them died for their faith. Acts chapter 7 gives a graphic story of the first such martyr whose name was Stephen. He never once complained. All through his ordeal, he prayed, and even asked God to forgive his persecutors.

The persecution of God's church will continue until Jesus finally delivers His people. Weeping may endure for a night, but joy comes in the morning. The redeemed will enter the city of which John spoke. For the first time the people of God will enjoy real uninterrupted joy and contentment (*Revelation 21: 21-23*).

Although Nebuchadnezzar had the command of his captives, he exercised much wisdom in dealing with them. He acted wisely in advising his servants to feed and educate the brightest young men among the captives. In choosing these young men to be educated in all matters concerning the kingdom, the king's decision though immediate would be to his long-term advantage.

These men would make valuable contributions to the efficient administration of his kingdom. Scripture says these young men were already skilful in wisdom, knowledge, and science, but their educational accomplishments were not enough to escape captivity. God was working His purpose out, and in time, they would understand. The song writer says," When you don't understand trust your heart." They were well favored in Babylon and they experienced royal treatment from their captors.

> Verse 6 Now among these were of the children of Judah, Daniel, Hananiah, Mishael, Azariah: 7 unto whom the prince of the eunuchs gave names: for he gave unto Daniel the name of Belteshazzar; and to Hananiah of Shadrach; and to Mishael Mishach; and to Azariah of Abednego (*Daniel* 1: 6, 7).

Daniel and his friends underwent a name change and the main reason for this change, was the spiritual meaning of their names. Daniel signifies, "Judge for God," Hananiah, "gift from God," Mishael, "who is what God is," Azariah, "whom Jehovah helps." Their new names had connections to heathen divinities and Chaldeans worship. Daniel's new name Belteshazzar "prince of Bel," Shadrach "servant of Sin," (the moon god); Meshach, "who is what Aku is." (Aku is the equivalent of Sin, and Abednego), "servant of Nebo." If the king thought name change would be mind change he was wrong.

Name change did not affect the loyalty these men had for God. They made up their minds to be true to their belief, actions and choice of food. God honored them by bringing them into tender love and favor with the prince of the eunuchs, and he allowed them to eat the diet they chose. Daniel encountered great temptations in Babylon, and he realized that he must keep his body under. "To make God's grace our own, we must act our part." "Here are revealed the conditions of success" (S.D.A. *Bible Commentary* Vol. 4, p. 1167).

God does honor those who honor Him. (*1Samuels* 2:30). Daniel knew that in order to be a victor, he must have clear mental perceptions that he might discern between right and wrong. While he was working on his part, God worked also, and gave him "knowledge and skill in all learning and wisdom: Daniel had understanding in all visions and dreams" (*Ibid.*, p. 1166).

Men must cooperate with God in carrying out His plan. If we do, what He has done for Daniel, He will do for us today. Daniel and his companions did not know what would be the result of their decisions. They were to make the most of their opportunities and use their time prudently for study and labor. While these young men were working out their own salvation, adhering to a strict path of temperance and obedience, God was working in them, both to will and to do of His good pleasure.

CHAPTER 6

Nebuchadnezzar's Perplexing Dream

In the days of the kings, dreams and visions were popular ways God used to communicate. Nebuchadnezzar had a dream but could not remember it. He therefore called for the wise men of Babylon to tell him the dream and the interpretation.

Verse two of Daniel 2 "Then the king commanded to call the magicians, and the astrologers, and sorcerers, and the Chaldeans, for to show the king his dreams. So they came and stood before the king."

The magicians used magic. They employed superstitious rites and fortunetelling, while the astrologers pretended to be adept in the study of the stars. The science of astrology including the practice of sorceries was used by Eastern nations. Sorcerers pretended to hold communication with the dead. The Chaldeans were an elite sect of philosophers consistent with the principles and practices of the magicians and astrologers who studied natural science and divinations. The king told his trusted men he did not remember the dream, so he wanted them to tell him the dream and the interpretation. They were astonished at the request Verse 4 "O king, live forever: tell thy servants the dream, and we will show the interpretation."

The thorough and stringent training of the magicians and astrologers caused them to illicit enough information to form a basis for some shrewd calculations. They would frame their answers in ambiguous ways that would be applicable wherever the turn of events led. It is for these reasons they asked the king to tell them the dream, they would then use cunning interpretation that would not endanger their reputation. They spoke to the king in Syriac a dialect of the Chaldean language, used by the learned educated class *(Daniel and the Revelation p . . . 22, 23)*.

> [5]The king said, "I can't recall the details. That's why I called you, to tell me the dream and interpret it for me. If you cannot, I will have you torn limb from limb and will turn your houses into garbage heaps.
>
> [6]On the other hand, if you tell me the dream and interpret it, I will give you gifts, rewards, and will greatly honor you. So tell me the dream and interpret it for me."
>
> [7] Once again they said to the king, "Your majesty, tell us the dream and we will be happy to interpret it for you."
>
> [8] The king asked, "Are you stalling for time to cover up the fact that you can't tell me the dream, hoping I will forget about it?
>
> [9] If you won't tell me the dream there's only one reason for it. You've agreed among yourselves to come up with an answer that pleases me, because I would have no way of knowing whether is true or not. So, you had better tell me the dream I had and interpret it for me now."
>
> [10] The men were afraid and said, "Your Majesty, There's no one on earth who can do what the king is asking. No ruler, no matter how great and mighty has ever demanded such a thing from his priests, fortune-tellers, and astrologers.

¹¹ What the king wants is impossible. No one can tell someone else what he dreamed except the gods, but they don't live among the people."

¹² This made the king very angry and he ordered all the wise men in Babylon executed.

¹³ As the death decree was being drawn up, the king's guards went out to find those who, for whatever reason, weren't able to come at the king's earlier command, including Daniel and his friends.

The guards were to take them to the place for execution along with the rest (*Daniel 2: 5-13 CW*).

These humble men of God attained the highest office in Babylon, and were now among the wise men of Babylon. Though they were included with those for execution, they were not like the Babylonian wise men; they feared and obeyed the God of heaven.

These above mentioned verses reveal the desperate struggle between the king and the wise men. The latter, now caught trying to be who they were not, were now seeking a way of escape, but the king insisted that they do what they claimed they could do and be true to their profession. On the surface, it would seem the king was unreasonable to expect the wise men to be able to tell the dream he had and could not remember. However, didn't the magicians claim to be able to reveal hidden things, to foretell events, to make known mysteries entirely beyond human wisdom, and to do this by the help of supernatural agencies?

Their further admission that only the gods whose dwelling is not with men could make known the matter was a way of saying they had no communication with these gods. Hence, they could do no more than their human knowledge and wisdom could reveal. This made the king extremely furious when he realized he was the victim of deception (*Ibid.* p. 24). At this point, he had no confidence in them, and accused them of lack of loyalty. His actions clearly said the only way he would believe their interpretation is if they could tell him the dream.

The king is afraid so he threatens to kill the wise men. Astrologers, Chaldeans and magicians received special schooling in the art of eliciting enough information about a matter and then constructing their answers in a dubious way that would be relevant whichever way the results turned. Could not these moments be the lowest point in Babylon's history that demonstrated the bankruptcy of its astrological system?"

Though the decision of the king was extreme, the men were imposters and some measures had to be employed to stop them. The word magicians featured greatly in the days of the kings of Egypt. Sadly though, these magicians could not interpret the king's dream.

> And it came to pass in the morning that his spirit was troubled; and he sent and called for all the magicians of Egypt, and all the wise men thereof: and Pharaoh told them his dream; but there was none that could interpret them unto the Pharaoh (*Genesis 41:8*).

Another reference is *Exodus 7:11* Aaron's rod became a snake and Pharaoh's magicians with enchantment did the same. They also imitated the first two plagues that came upon Egypt but was unable to imitate the third. They, in chapter 8: 19 advised the king that the third plague was the finger of God.

Arioch the captain of the king's guard went for Daniel and his friends to take them to the place of execution. Daniel was astonished and wanted to know why he was in so much haste. Arioch explained the matter and Daniel wasted no time but went in and desired time of the king, so he could show him the interpretation. Daniel then informed his friends of the decision of the king, and together they sought God's intervention.

(*Daniel* 2: 17-19) Then Daniel went to his house, and made the thing known to Hananiah, Mishael, and Azariah, his companions: [18] That they would desire mercies of the God of heaven, concerning this secret; that Daniel and his fellows should not perish with the rest of the wise men of Babylon. [19] Then was the secret revealed unto Daniel in a night vision. Then Daniel blessed the God of heaven.

Of the four Hebrews, God chose to give Daniel wisdom to interpret all kinds of dreams. Dreams and visions were favorite fields of study in Babylon. Consequently, the ability of the Babylonians to interpret dreams, was highly recognized in Babylon even though they did so by divination.

On the other hand, true dreams and their interpretations are forms of divine revelation. Daniel's ability to interpret dreams was because of his prayer life, dedication, and faithfulness to God. Daniel and his friends were professional advisors to the king, and would be killed with the other wise men.

Their success earned them the right to become members of the group of the wise men of Babylon, though for whatever reason they were not included in the initial group who went before the king. It is also hardly likely that the magicians and astrologers would have shared with Daniel and his friends, the rewards the king would have given, if they were successful in satisfying the king's requests. Yet Daniel told the king not to destroy them "They were saved because there was a man of God among them." (*Ibid*, p.28).

Pray when storm clouds gather about you
Pray, light will shine through.

Daniel did just that and God answered his prayer. Here is the difference between divination and divine interpretation. The God of heaven had answered Daniel's prayer, and he offered praise and thanks to the God of heaven for revealing the dream.

> (*Verses 20-23 of Daniel*) He said[20] "Praise God forever and ever. All wisdom and power are His: [21] He changes times and the seasons, He removes kings and sets up kings. He gives wisdom to those who are wise, and insight and understanding to those who know Him. [22] He reveals mysteries that no one else can know and He sees what to man is hidden in darkness. He's the source of all knowledge, and He floods the world with all the light of understanding.[23] O Lord, God of my fathers, I thank You and praise You for giving insight and wisdom and courage to go in and see the king. You've answered my prayers and given me the dream and told me what it means. Now I can go in and tell the king what he wants to know.

Like Daniel, we should offer thanks giving to God for the things He has done for us, and for answering our petitions. "Let no mercy from the hand of God fail of its due return of thanksgiving and praise" (*Daniel and the Revelation p.26*).

Another noteworthy quality in Daniel was that although God revealed the dream to him, he included his companions by referring to the answer as, "what we desired of Thee" (*Ibid.* p. 26). After receiving revelation from God about the dream and its interpretations, Daniel then hurried to break the news to Arioch, and asked him not to destroy the wise men of Babylon. "Bring me before the king," he said, "and I will show unto the king the interpretation" (*Daniel 2:24*). Arioch's opening sentence to the king, revealed a sharp contrast between himself and Daniel. He said, "I have found a man of the captives of Judah that will make known unto the king the interpretation" (*verse 25*).

Whereas Daniel shared the results of the answered dream with his friends, Arioch claimed to have found a man. Arioch's representations to the king possibly was to have the king believe he was the one searching for an interpreter and had found one at last. Did Arioch not know that Daniel had gone to see the king, or did he think the king would have forgotten he had seen him?

Nebuchadnezzar was about to encounter the God of heaven and earth, through the discourse with Daniel and his friends. As Daniel entered into the royal palace, the king's question to him was, "Art thou able to make known unto me the dream which I have seen and the interpretation thereof?" (*verse 26*). To the king Daniel seemed so young and inexperienced, how could he make known a matter that his experienced magicians, soothsayers, astrologers, and wise men could not do?

Daniel lost no time in telling the king that the matter was beyond their power hence, the king should not be angry with them nor think anything of their vain superstitions. Daniel went on to exalt the God of heaven as the only revealer of secrets, and He will make known to the king what will take place in the last days. Daniel struck a key note in exalting God over his limitations.

He took no credit for himself, and sought to temper the king's pride in praising and acknowledging the God of heaven. He informed him that although he had the dream, it was not for his sake alone he received the interpretation, but for those through whom it should be given. (*Ibid.* p.28).

One of the reasons God gave Nebuchadnezzar the dream was, he was a futuristic king, and God granted him his desire by giving him this prophetic dream (*Daniel and the Revelation p. 28*). God was working through His servant Daniel who was of more value in His sight than were the kings of earth. The act of revealing the dream to Daniel accomplished many other providential works of God. His servants were exalted in their eyes.

- He made the king aware of the things he desired to know.
- God saved His servants who trusted in Him.
- In a very conspicuous way, he brought before the Chaldeans, the knowledge of the One who knows the end from the beginning.
- He exposed the false systems of the soothsayers and magicians.
- He honored His own name.
- His servants were exalted in their eyes. (*Ibid.* p. 29 paraphrase).

> *Verse* [29] "As for thee, O king, thy thoughts came into thy mind upon thy bed, what should come to pass hereafter: and He that revealeth secrets maketh known to thee what shall come to pass.
> [30] But as for me this secret is not revealed to me for any wisdom that I have more than any living, but for their sakes that shall make known the interpretation to the king, and that thou mightest know the thoughts of thy head.

Unlike many of his counterparts, who were only interested in the present, Nebuchadnezzar thought of the future and was anxious to know the events that would occur in the future.

> It was partly for this reason that God gave him this dream, which we must regard as a token of divine favor to the king.
> Yet God would not work for the king independently of his own people. Though He gave the dream to the king He sent the interpretation through one of His acknowledged servants.[4]

Obedient May speak Freely

Daniel was true to God, and God honored him. We all should learn from Daniel, that God honors those who honor Him. If we seek the kingdom of God first, He will add other blessings to us. In the experience of Daniel, his spiritual and intellectual

> In the faithful discharge of duty we may become one with Christ; for those who are obeying God's commands may speak to Him freely.

capabilities developed proportionately. He laid all his difficulties before God. He ignored ridicule and he developed a serene and cheerful way of life. His taxing duties were made light because he brought the light and love of God into his work.

> Those who live in close fellowship with Christ will be promoted by Him to positions of trust. The servant who does the best he can for His master, is admitted to familiar intercourse with one whose commands he loves to obey. In the faithful discharge of duty, we may become one with Christ; for those who are obeying God's commands may speak to Him freely. The one who talks more familiarly with His divine Leader has the most exalted conception of His greatness, and is the most obedient to His commands. [5]

---

[4]   Treasures of Life p.28.
[5]   S.D. A. Bible Commentary on Daniel 2, Vol., 4, p 1168.

CHAPTER 7

Revelation and Interpretation
of the Dream

After explaining to the king that the "God of heaven" gave him the dream to let him know "what shall be in the latter days," Daniel proceeded to relate the dream.

> *Daniel 2:31-34* In the vision you saw an enormous statue of a man. The statue, glowed with a brilliant light and as it stood before you, it was frightening to look at. [32] The head of the statute was made of fine gold, its chest and arms of silver, its waist and hips of bronze, [33] its legs of iron and his feet partly iron and partly clay. [34] While you were looking at it, you saw a huge rock broke loose from a mountain without anyone touching it, and strike the statue on his feet of iron and clay, smashing them to pieces *(CW)*.

To Nebuchadnezzar an idol worshiper, the idea of an image would appeal to his senses. God in His wisdom used this vivid representation to bring needed truth to the king. For the benefit of His people, God would show to Nebuchadnezzar the emptiness and worthlessness of earthly monarchs. Silver, brass, iron, and the mixture of iron and clay followed the head of gold.

Finally, the entire image was dashed to pieces and was scattered by the wind.

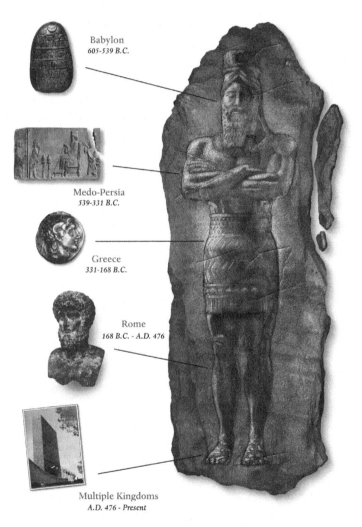

Babylon
605-539 B.C.

Medo-Persia
539-331 B.C.

Greece
331-168 B.C.

Rome
168 B.C. - A.D. 476

Multiple Kingdoms
A.D. 476 - Present

(The Image of Nebuchadnezzar's dream)

www.Goodsalt.com

This once impressive image will dissipate and a kingdom more durable and of heavenly origin take its place. God will show to men that earthly kingdoms are temporary and will pass away. The earthly greatness of men will burst like bubbles. The positions so long usurped by earthly monarchs will vanish away. God will set up His kingdom that will have no end and all who love His appearing will dwell with Him in peace forever and ever.

> *Verse 36.* This is the dream: and we will tell the interpretation thereof before the king. [37] Thou O king, art a king of kings: for the God of heaven hath given thee a kingdom, power, and strength and glory.
> [38] And wheresoever the children of men dwell, the beast of the field and the fowls of the heaven, hath He given into thy hand, and hath made thee ruler over them all. Thou art this head of gold.

One of the most comprehensive histories of the world's empire was now about to be opened by the interpretation of this dream. Just eight verses, but they encompass the rise and fall of nations. These verses would change the world forever. They speak to the setting up and falling of empires, past cycles and ages, past our day, to the eternal state. A unique prediction, very comprehensive, yet so minute, that it represents the rule of earthly kingdoms from that time, to our time (*Daniel & the Revelation* p.31 paraphrased).

It is beyond human reasoning to devise so brief yet all embracing phenomenon. This is the finger of God and it would do us good to take heed. Daniel informed the king that God had made him ruler over his entire kingdom. This mention was to prevent him from thinking he was the one that by his own power had attained that honor.

The interpretation of the dream, in its minutest detail convinced the king that this was divine revelation. These solemn truths made deep impressions on his mind, and in humility and reverence, he fell on his face and worshipped. He saw clearly the difference between the wisdom of God and those of the most intelligent men in his kingdom.

God had favored the king of Babylon by allowing gold to represent his kingdom. Nebuchadnezzar's actions proved he was not satisfied to be just the head of gold. He wanted the entire image to be gold. (*Ibid.* p.36). What he did next was direct defiance of the wisdom and authority of God. He wanted more than part gold, and he wanted his kingdom to last forever. He would show every one his kingdom was not going to be just the head of gold. He built a huge image of gold from head to toes sixty cubits tall and six cubits wide (approximately 100 feet by 10 feet). To continue his contempt for the authority of God, he set a day when all the people under his jurisdiction would pay homage and bow to this impressive image in the act of its dedication.

The king's actions were not unique, nor were they bolder than some of our actions today. We defy God's instructions in many of the choices we make. God gave us the Bible as our guide and road map. However, many people offer service to Him contrary to His instructions. They determine what they will follow and what they will discard. Let those who decide to add and subtract from the word of God take heed. "Don't add anything or take anything away from His instructions, but stay with what the law says and obey the commandments as I have given them to you *(Deut. 4:2, CW)*. Remember God is particular.

God allowed Daniel and the other faithful witnesses to be among the other captives taken to Babylon to carry light to the dark practices of heathenism and idolatry. Ezra and Nehemiah were witnesses for God in their captivity. God had scattered them abroad among many heathen nations to be His witnesses. Is God still allowing this to be the experience of His people in these days? Yes He is. Just follow reports from volunteers from Maranatha, ADRA, ASI, 3ABN, Mother Teresa, to name a few. The people, who have gone to remote areas of our world, may not have been taken as captives, but they have volunteered to be captives for Jesus. They trade comfort, for primitive living in order to let their light shine for Jesus among people who know little or nothing about Him.

God had chosen Daniel to reflect the light of heaven on the proud kingdom of Babylon. The king now realized that the God of heaven was the Ruler over all kings of the earth. Just as how Daniel and his companions reflected the light from heaven and allowed God to occupy "Center Stage" in their lives, He expects His faithful witnesses to shine forth the true light from heaven in these last days and give Him "Center Stage" in their lives. If the saints of Old Testament times, could dare to stand up for Jesus, how much more should the saints now who, have the accumulated light of many centuries of faithful watchmen, stand up for Jesus and be counted.

Ellen White in *Great Controversy* p. 351, says "The spirit that does not cause us to live soberly, righteously, and godly, in this present world is not the Spirit of Christ." Paul says in *2 Corinthians* 13: 5 "Examine yourselves, whether ye be in the faith; prove your own selves. Know ye not your own selves, how that Jesus Christ is in you, except ye be reprobates?"

With Jesus, though your sins be as scarlet He can make them white as snow. Jesus does not ask us to do the "clean up" job, He will. He is the only one who knows how to use red blood to make hearts white.

Chapter 8

Magnificent Babylon

The Babylonian empire came to power under Nabopolassar the father of Nebuchadnezzar. He ruled two years conjointly with his son, and after his death in **604 B.C.**, Nebuchadnezzar began to reign (*Daniel and the Revelation* p.21). When he took the throne he was already physically and mentally strong. He was a soldier, architect, and political leader; and was soon to become the greatest man of his time.

Babylon's origin

Nimrod the great grandson of Noah founded the kingdom of Babylon, more than two thousand years before Christ. The head of gold represented this Babylon. Nimrod the mighty hunter built Babel (*Genesis 10: 8-10*) and many believed he founded Nineveh, which later became the capital of Assyria.

Babylon was a golden kingdom situated in the garden of the East. It was a square city about sixty miles in circumference, with a wall about three hundred feet high, and seven feet thick. Sixty miles of moat fortified the outer wall. Thirty miles of river wall passed through its center, and its gates were of solid brass. The hanging gardens equaled the height of the walls of its two royal palaces. The circumference of its Belus temple was three miles, and its subterranean tunnel under the River Euphrates connected its palaces. This splendid city had many wonders of the world. The head of gold in the great historic image of Nebuchadnezzar's dream represented this magnificent city (*Treasures of Life* p.33, paraphrased).

> The magnificent multi towered Ishtar Gate, still the most impressive ruin in Babylon, was covered with blue-glazed bricks, with bulls and dragons in relief. The wide Procession Street passing through the gate connected important temples and palaces of the city and was the scene of many colorful festival procession . . . The famous building known as the Hanging Gardens of Babylon forms part of the palace area.[6]

The comparison of antiquated cities showed Babylon to be the largest and greatest of them. It is not a wonder then that Nebuchadnezzar boasted about the great Babylon that he built. They considered Babylon the religious center of the world, and as such, the city was without rival. The Babylonians regarded their city as the "naval" of the world, because the sanctuary of the god Marduk, (who they considered lord of heaven and earth) was there.

The following inscription now in the Berlin Museum, speaks to the pride Nebuchadnezzar felt for his accomplishments. "I have made Babylon, the holy city, the glory of the great gods, more prominent than before, and have promoted its rebuilding. I have caused the sanctuaries of gods and goddesses to lighten up like the day"

(Ibid., p. 799).

Etemenanki the famous temple of Babylon its pride and joy, was 299 feet (91 m.) square at the base. Its height was 300 feet (91.4 m. high)

(*Bible Commentary* p.797). At the time of Nebuchadnezzar, there were more than 50 temples, 955 small sanctuaries, 384 street-alters and all of them were within the city.

> O Babylon whosoever beholds thee is filled with rejoicing,
> Whosoever dwells in Babylon increases his life,
> Whosoever speaks evil of Babylon is like one who kills his own mother.
> Babylon is like a sweet date palm, whose fruit is lovely to behold."
> An ancient song of praise (as given by E. Ebeling Keilschrifttexte
> Aus Assur religiösen Inhalts, *[Leipzig, 1915], No. 8):(Ibid).*

Such was Babylon, with Nebuchadnezzar in the prime of life, bold, vigorous and accomplished. He was the reigning monarch, when Daniel went to Babylon and served as a captive for seventy years in its gorgeous palace. Despite the dazzling beauty of Babylon, these captives of Israel were not happy. Neither were they thrilled to witness the idolatrous worship of pagan gods instead of the True God. It is not surprising the people of God could not play their harps in the land of their captivity, but hung them on the willows by the Euphrates, and wept at the thought of Zion their homeland (*Ps.* 137:1-4).

The image represented a deterioration of succeeding kingdoms of the earth, in power and glory. This prophetic image also shows the decline of morality and religion among the people of these kingdoms. Every succeeding kingdom was worst than the one it succeeded.

- One of the reasons Babylon passed away was the rulers attributed its prosperity to human accomplishments, instead of giving God the glory.

- The kingdom of Medo Persia was visited because they trampled God's law under foot. The actions of the people were corrupt, blasphemous, and wicked. The fear of God had no place in them.
- The kingdoms after them were worst than they, they cast away all allegiance to God and sank lower in the quagmire of corruption, and degradation.
- The iron and clay feet of the image represent a mingling of churchcraft and state. Take note that the transference of power from the state to the church will bring devastating results; it happened before and will happen again. God's people must not build on the foundation of wood, hay and stubble, He desires His people to have sanctified discernment.

Those loyal to the commandment of God will uphold the distinguishing feature of our faith that is the proclamation of the Everlasting Gospel/the Three Angels Message of *Revelation* 14: 6-12. If governments would obey the commandment of God as He commands, they would stand in the strength of God and defend the faith given to the saints. However, they will instead obey the spurious sabbath in allegiance to the papacy, but God will one day punish those who have made void His law.

Daniel 2: Nebuchadnezzar's reign of forty-three years, was succeeded by the following:

1. His son, Evil Merodach, who reigned for **two** years.
2. His son-in-law, Neriglssar, who reigned for **four** years.
3. Neriglassar's son, Laborosoarchod, reigned **nine** months (which was not counted in Ptolemy because it was less than one year)
4. Nabonidus, whose son, Belshazzar, grandson to Nebuchadnezzar was a close associate to him on his throne,

History records that Nabonidus married to the daughter of Nebuchadnezzar who fathered Belshazzar, in his fifteenth year of his reign.

[6]   *S. D. A. Bible Commentary Vol., 4, p.799*

CHAPTER 9

Rise and Fall of the Image Kingdoms

The Babylonians and the Medes had war only two years after the death of Nebuchadnezzar which was during the reign of Neriglassar. Darius of the Medes, invited Cyrus of Persia to join him in the fight, and they had uninterrupted success until the eighteenth year of Nabonidus, which was the third year of Belshazzar.

Babylon (B.C.605-539.)

The Babylonians felt safe within their impregnable walls with enough provisions to last for at least twenty years, and enough land within the city wall to produce enough food for everyone for an indefinite period. They scoffed at Cyrus from their high walls, and mocked at their futile effort to get in, and bring them into subjection.

Based on these logical human thinking they had reasons to feel safe. Hence, they slept soundly and went about their normal daily routine, as though there was no enemy on the outside of the wall trying to get in. It would appear that Babylon was invincible, but the clock of prophecy was ticking prophetic time away and proud Babylon would come down from his throne of glory.

Their feeling of security worked to their ruin because Cyrus was determined to use stratagem to accomplish what force was unable to accomplish. His day of attack would be on the Babylonians annual festival where the whole city would be celebrating through mirth and revelry. The only way he could enter the city was via the Euphrates River at the point where it passed under the walls.

Cyrus divided his men in three groups and placed them at strategic points. One group was to re-channel the river into a large artificial lake just above the city, which would be used as their passage to enter the city. The second group was to be at the point where the river entered the city; the third group was to be fifteen miles down stream where the river emerged from the city. The two latter groups were to make their way to the point of the palace and take the guards by surprise and kill them.[7]

All this effort would have been in vain if the careless, drunken guards had barred and guarded the inner gates of the city as they usually did. Isaiah the prophet in chapter 45 verse1 foretold this event.

> Thus saith thee Lord to His anointed, to Cyrus whose right
> hand I have holden, to subdue nations before him; and I will
> lose the loins of kings, to open before him the two leaved gates;
> and the gates shall not be shut.

The entrance of the Persians went undetected. No one realized that the water level was going down; neither did they see the Persian soldiers stealing a march on them. That night's wild and reckless debauchery cost the Babylonians their freedom and kingdom. When Belshazzar realized what was happening, it was too late, and he died fighting for his life. Cyrus besieged Babylon which was the only country in the east that had withstood them. *Isaiah* 13:19-22 says Babylon would not be rebuilt. Thus was the chapter of Babylon symbolized by the head of gold, closed, and a country inferior to Babylon, the Medes and Persians symbolized by silver, the breast and arms of the great image came into being.

Medio-Persian Kingdom (B.C. 539-331.)

This kingdom was inferior in wealth, magnificence, and luxury compared to Babylon, but was more impressive in power, for it conquered Babylon, and subdued the entire East from the Aegean Sea to the River Indus and formed a more extensive empire. From a Biblical standpoint, the Babylonians under king Nebuchadnezzar captured Israel and took them to Babylon. Years later, Cyrus king of the Medes restored them to their own land. As an act of courtesy in **538 B. C.,** Cyrus gave his uncle Darius, the highest office in the kingdom. However, Darius died two years later, leaving Cyrus the sole monarch of this new empire.

History was again to play an important role in the life of Cyrus, for this year ended Israel's seventy years (**70**) of captivity in Babylon. Cyrus gave his famous decree for the Jews to return to their homeland, and to start the rebuilding of the temple destroyed by the Babylonians during the siege of Jerusalem. This was to be the first installment of the great decree for the **restoration** and **rebuilding** of Jerusalem (see *Ezra* 6: 14) and was completed in **457 B.C.** during the reign of Artaxerxes.

Cyrus reigned seven years and left the kingdom to his son, Cambyses who reigned seven years and five months to **522 B.C.** Between this time and **336 B.C.**, ten monarchs reigned. The last of the Persian kings to reign, came on the scene in **335 B. C.**

His name Darius Condomannus who was a noble man, with a mild and generous disposition, but no qualification could make him successful, in the contest he was about to face. Just as how the Medes and Persians being an inferior kingdom to Babylon overthrew the Babylonians, so an inferior kingdom was about to overthrow them.

Scarcely was he warm on his throne, when Alexander the head of the Greek soldiers attacked him. The third kingdom was about to enter the world stage. The Grecians defeated the Persians in the field of Arbela in **331 B.C.,** and Alexander became the exclusive ruler over the Persian Empire in such a degree never before experienced by the Empire.[8]

Grecian Empire (B.C.331-168.)

Greece was now the third universal empire of the earth. The brutal slaying Darius by three of his subjects, brought Alexander to tears at the sight of the sad spectacle of the lifeless body of Darius, killed by his own men and left by the side of the roadway. Alexander threw his coat over the body, and then commanded the soldiers to convey his body to the royal palace of Persia. He also paid the funeral expenses. With Darius out of the way, Alexander had no known enemy, so he spent his time in pleasure seeking and some minor conquests.

He was an arrogant man and claimed for himself divine honors. He was an out of control drinker and would sometimes murder his friends and favorites in his drunken frenzies. He encouraged excessive drinking among his soldiers, and on one occasion twenty of them died because of their carousal. Once having engaged in a drinking spree he was invited to one drinking session after another of his drinking buddies and after drinking to each of his twenty guests, two Herculean cups, (a cup contains six quarts) he was seized with a violent fever, and died eleven days later, **June 13, 323 B.C.,** in his thirty-second year of life.[9]

The fourth kingdom will be strong as iron. Just as iron can crush all metals, so it will crush everything that stands in its way but it will be still more base and corrupt *(Daniel 2: 40)*.

Iron Monarchy of Rome (B.C.168.-. A.D.476.)

The fourth division of the image was the legs of iron, represented by the kingdom of Rome who conquered Greece. At the opening of the Christian era, this empire ruled all Europe, which included, France, the greater part of the Netherlands, Switzerland, south of Germany, Hungary, Turkey, Greece and Asia. One writer says, 'Rome filled the world.' This was a period where Rome made laws that affected everyone. There was nowhere to go, and to resist, could mean death. Rome was strong but divided. Daniel also predicted this prophecy.[10]

Verse 41. "This kingdom will split into ten parts represented by the ten toes some of these little kingdoms will be strong and others will be weak, just as the toes were made partly of iron and partly of clay."

Rome Divided Multiple Kingdoms (A.D. 476-Present)

The presence of clay in the feet and toes represented an element of weakness. Prior to the division of Rome into ten kingdoms, she lost the iron strength, which she possessed earlier in the first centuries of her existence. The destroyer of nations and individuals now seem out of control with effeminacy, and degeneracy due to her luxury. Rome now weakened, became vulnerable and her power and strength were at low ebb. This then prepared the way for its disintegration into ten kingdoms. According to prophecy, the toes represent the ten final divisions or kingdoms of the image of Nebuchadnezzar.

There is a parallel between the image of Daniel 2, and the beasts of chapter 7. The fourth beast represents the same kingdom, as does the iron legs of the image. The ten toes of the image are similar to the ten horns of the beast. These horns clearly depict the ten independent kingdoms, which should arise. They would not be successive kings or kingdoms because the little horn annihilated three of them. The ten horns represent the ten divided kingdoms. In the interpretation of the image, Daniel uses the words "kings," and "kingdoms," interchangeably.

In verse 44, Daniel says "And in the days of these kings" . . . God would set up His kingdom during the reign of the kings represented by the toes, that is during the reign of the divided kingdoms of the Roman Empire.

This division happened between the years **A.D. 351** and **A.D. 476**. The Barbarian tribes of Western Europe and North Africa brought the Roman Empire to their knees in **A.D. 476**. These Barbarian tribes then became the modern nations of Western Europe. Each of these tribes (with the exception of three which are now extinct), had sizeable portions of the Roman territory, as independent and separate kingdoms. These kingdoms are as follows:

Alemanni : Germans	**Anglo-Saxons** : British
Visigoths : Spanish	**Lombards** : Italians
Franks : French	**Burgundians** : Swiss
Suevi : Portuguese	**Heruli** : extinct
Ostrogoths : extinct	**Vandals** : extinct

These nations represented by the toes, would according to the dream, try to "mingle themselves with the seed of men" (*Daniel 2:43*). In essence, they were trying to re-establish the unity that was lost when the Western Roman Empire collapsed. This hope of re-unification of the Western Roman Empire is a dream that has failed repeatedly.

European monarchs tried intermarriage but failed miserably. The intention of intermarriage was to avert conflict and promote peace among these nations, but this could not happen, because the word of God said they would not cleave. There is still disunity, among these shattered kingdoms.

The dawn of the twentieth century revealed that every high-ranking hereditary ruler was family to the British Royal family. The First World War proved how futile that attempt was. President Woodrow Wilson, said, "The world has been made safe for democracy!" *(Daniel and the Revelation p.51)* What paradox to think that a war brings peace, this is great fallacy, and is similar to an attempt to use fire to put out fire.

Laws are useless if they are inactive. Therefore, laws must be activated in order to achieve their intended results. It is immoral for anyone to break constitutional laws, but even worst when the makers of these laws are the breakers. The world league of nations was formed to restrain dictators and punish aggressors, yet close to the palace of the League of Nations, leaders were destroying peace, and shattering the plans of world union, and at the same time were preaching social revolution. Once again bear in mind that the prophecy represented by the feet part iron and clay, indicate both strength and weakness. Hence, the promise of purporting right, "partly strong" and doing otherwise, "partly broken," was again fulfilling prophecy.[11]

"They shall not cleave"

Charles the V tried to unify Europe but came under pressure to resign. Louis XIV of France attempted. Napoleon tried force, but it did not work, so he tried to use alliance to build up one mighty, consolidated empire but it too it did not work. Charlemagne, Kaiser Wilhelm, and Hitler tried, but they all failed miserably because God told Daniel that, "they shall not cleave one to another." *(More on Charlemagne see Appendix A)*

The word of God will not return to Him void, the strength and ambition of man cannot change the plan of God. The mixture of iron and clay, will not cleave together. The combination of iron and clay is impossible. When God says seven, six will not be acceptable. He says,

"Thus says the Lord," He will not accept what man tries to alter and twist to suit his convenience.

These kingdoms experienced partial strength and weakness, early in their inception. Three kingdoms succumbed to devastation, and it was thus "broken," and will continue to be non-existent. Rome was the last of the world's universal empires, and when Rome fell, no single earthly kingdom would rule the world.

For more than 1500 years, the destiny of the Western world was controlled by the simple but prophetic words. Europe will never reunite into the Western Roman Empire, because God said it would not happen. Man's feeble attempt to unite these nations will continue to fail. The only power that can unite the nations and the world is the kingdom of God represented by the great stone of Nebuchadnezzar's dream. [12]

Daniel & the Revelation (paraphrased portions)

[7]   Ibid, pp. 37, 38

[8]   Ibid, pp. 41, 42

[9]   Ibid, p 43

[10] Ibid, p.45

[11] Ibid, p.47

[12] Ibid, pp. 49-52

CHAPTER 10

The Stone that Filled the World

All the predictions concerning the image happened right on time. Its inferior, the Medes and Persians, defeated Babylon. Greece defeated Medo Persia and Rome defeated Greece. There is but one remaining kingdom represented by the Stone that filled the whole earth. This kingdom will not be defeated, nor would anyone succeed it. This is characteristic of God's kingdom. God said it and He means it.

(The Stone that destroys the Image)
www.Goodsalt.com

Isaiah 55:11 says, "So the words that go out of my mouth will not return to me empty but will carry out my wishes and succeed in what I sent it out to do" (*CW*).

Matthew 25:31 supports this statement, "When the Son of Man shall come in His glory, and all the holy angels with Him, and then shall He sit upon the throne of His glory." We are now living in the period represented by the toes of the image.

> (*Daniel* 2: 44) The time will come when all kingdoms of the world will try to work together. That is when the God of heaven will decide to set up His kingdom, which will destroy all kingdoms of the world. God's kingdom will never be conquered or destroyed and will stand forever [45] In your dream, Your Majesty, you saw how a huge rock broke loose from a mountain without anyone touching it and struck the statue on his feet of iron and clay. You saw the statue fall do and the rock roll over the iron, bronze, silver, and gold turning them into dust. God is telling you ahead of time what will happen to these kingdoms. This is the dream and the interpretation that you asked for . . . (*CW*).

In the KJ, the word "shall," substitutes "will." This like other prophecies is sure, and will happen as God said. The kingdom of God will be the beginning of a new dispensation, where happiness and joy will replace sadness and gloom. Glory will replace disrepute and life will replace death. "When shall this kingdom be set up?"

Jesus said clearly in the book of *Matthew* 26: 29 at the last supper that, He would not drink with His disciples again until He drinks with them in His Father's kingdom. It means then that the kingdom would be future. *Acts 1:6* attests to that fact that Jesus did not set up this kingdom before He went back to heaven. Just before He went back to heaven, His disciples asked Him if He would restore the kingdom of Israel. The following texts confirm He would not. The kingdom that would be set up would not be left to men to be corrupted by them *1 Corinthians 15; 50* states that flesh and blood cannot inherit the kingdom.

James 2:5 makes it clear that the kingdom is for the faithful, those who love God, and *Luke 12: 32* says it for the little flock, and this flock by Luke's account in *Acts* 14: 22, must endure much tribulation and then enter into the kingdom of God. This kingdom recorded by *2 Timothy 1:4* is to be set up when Jesus shall judge the living and the dead. This according to *Matthew 25: 31-34*, is the time when Jesus shall come in His glory with all His holy angels.

All the prophecies of Daniel 2 have already happened, except for the stone cut out from the mountain, which will fill the world, which signifies the return of Christ. We do not know the exact time He will come, but signs just before He comes are fast fulfilling. The important question is, "Are you ready for His appearing?" "Is your lamp trimmed and burning?" His coming should be the most important message on our lips. Once again, are you ready for Jesus to come? If not, why not?

CHAPTER 11

The Golden Image

The image is a symbol, used by God to communicate to the king Nebuchadnezzar and the people what should happen to the nations of earth. However, he misinterpreted and rejected the interpretation that Daniel gave him. Nebuchadnezzar was about to make it into the self-glorification of his might and power. He summoned all the people of his domain, including governors, sheriffs, judges, counselors, captains, and rulers to come to the dedication of the image. His plan of action would hinder the propagation of the knowledge God desired the world to receive. Satan was working hard to thwart God's plan for humankind. He knows that uncontaminated truth, that is truth without error, is powerful and able to save.

Nebuchadnezzar built a statue sixty cubits high and six cubits in breath. This imposing statue of gold occupied a prominent spot in Dura. Idol worship was not new to Babylon, but this statue was one of its kind and its introduction was as an object of worship. Should this image gain prominence, it would be the established form of idol worship. If the

Hebrews were to bow to this image, they would defeat the purpose God intended them to fulfill, that is, of being a blessing to the heathen nation. [13]

As Nebuchadnezzar prepared to celebrate. The powers of darkness seemed on high alert to celebrate, the victory of the worship of the golden image. This commemoration would eulogize idolatry as the state religion of Babylon, and Nebuchadnezzar would triumph in his bid for self-glorification. God had three faithful sons who would lift the banner of Prince Emmanuel high, and declare to all the people present, that God was the King of kings, and to Him only would they bow.

He advised them to fall and worship the image when they hear the sound of music. Everyone bowed except, Shadrach, Meshach, and Abednego. They were to face the king who was angry that they disobeyed him and did not bow down to the golden image he made. He told them he was going to have the music again, and if they did not bow, he would throw them into a fiery furnace, and he went on, "and who is that god that shall deliver you out of my hand?"

Very fearlessly but respectfully, the young men told him they were not careful to answer him on the matter. They said further if it is so, their God whom they serve is able to deliver them, from the burning fiery furnace and He would deliver them out of his hand. However, if that were not God's plan to deliver them, they still would not serve his gods, nor worship the image, which he set up.

At those words, Nebuchadnezzar's countenance changed and he became very furious. In his rage, he commanded the furnace to heated seven times more than it was before. He then ordered the powerful men in his army to tie them up and cast them into the fire. These men with their hands tied fell in the fire unhurt, but those who threw them into the fire were burned by the intense heat pouring from the furnace. [14]

The king noticed that there was a fourth person in the fire, and acknowledged that the form of the Fourth is like the Son of God. He called the heroes out and blessed the name of the God of Shadrach, Meshach, and Abednego, who had sent His angels and delivered His servants that trusted in Him. Their actions changed the king's words. These men gave their bodies that they may not serve and worship any other god but the God of heaven.

He went further to make a decree that if anyone said any thing about the God of the Hebrews, their house would become dunghills, because no other god can deliver as their God can. Daniel and these young men had lived careful, disciplined lives there in Babylon. They spoke about the Son of God and expounded as to the knowledge of the True and Living God, who is ruler of all things. Because of their lives and testimony, Nebuchadnezzar was able to recognize Jesus in the fire.

Believers in Christ, our circumstances may change, but we should remain faithful to God. He does not change, and He has promised to never leave us nor forsake us. He has done it for Daniel and these young men and He will do for us.

There is also the example of Joseph, who was mistreated by his brothers, sold as a slave and lied on by his master's wife. He spent years in prison for something he did not do. The butler who promised to remember him to the king forgot. Did he not have reasons to be bitter?

Of course, he did, but he valued his relationship with God, and God blessed him to the point of him becoming second highest in position in the country. He did it for them He will do it for you and me. Do not succumb to your sorrows, Jesus will bid them depart and He will deliver you.

The temptations will not last forever, but the effects, if we yield will be lasting. Do not yield to intimidation, each victory will make the next easier. Call on the name of Jesus, stand like a brave and He will carry you through.

These faithful young men yielded their natural abilities and unique intellectual culture to the sanctifying influence of divine grace. By their courageous actions, the power of the Divine Majesty of God was revealed to the vast assembly.

The presence of Jesus convinced the proud king, that it could be no other but the "Son of God". The glorious light from heaven was shining on Daniel and his friends, until all their associates understood the faith, which characterized their lives and beautified their character. It was not easier for these to be faithful than it is for us today. Stand up and be counted, even if you are the last one standing.

The Song Writer George Duffield, pens

> Stand up! Stand up for Jesus! Ye soldiers of the cross;
> Lift high His royal banner; It must not suffer loss;
> From victory unto victory, His army shall He lead,
> Till every foe is vanquished, And Christ is Lord indeed.
>
> Stand up! Stand up for Jesus! Stand in His strength alone;
> The arm of flesh will fail you; ye dare not trust your own.
> Put on the gospel armor and watching unto prayer,
> Where duty calls or danger, Be never wanting there.
>
> Stand up! Stand up for Jesus! The strife will not be long;
> This day the noise of battle, the next the victor's song.
> To him that overcometh, a crown of life shall be;
> He with the King of glory shall reign eternally.

God does not compel anyone to obey Him; He gives us free choice, to choose whom we will serve. The deliverance of these men showed that God stands with the oppressed, and remonstrates with all powers on earth that rebel against the authority of Heaven. These three young men demonstrated to the people of Babylon, their faithfulness and belief in

God. They were not afraid what man can do, because they relied on the unchanging word of God.

> Don't be afraid, I have redeemed you. I have named you. You are mine! When you walk through deep waters, I will be with you. When you walk through swollen rivers, they will not flow over you. When you walk through fire, you will not be burned; neither will the flame harm you *(Isaiah 4 3: 1, 2 CW)*.

The promise given to these men is available to us today. Stand up for Jesus. Do not fear man who can only hurt the body, rather fear God who can kill both body and soul in hell *(Luke* 12:5).

[13]   Prophets& Kings pp. 505, 506.

[14]   Bible Commentary Bk. 4 p.1169.

CHAPTER 12

Nebuchadnezzar's Second Dream

If the people of God live to please Him, even the heathen cannot but confess the name and goodness of God (*Philippians* 2: 10, 11). The king was now confessing the name of Jesus. He addressed the nations, people and languages, and admitted that God had showed him great signs and wonders, and that His kingdom is an everlasting kingdom. His dominion is from generation to generation. He admitted that the skill and wisdom of Daniel far exceeded that of his astrologers, magicians, soothsayers and Chaldeans of Babylon. He acknowledged the power of God manifested in His servant Daniel.[15]

For the second time Nebuchadnezzar had a dream and he who terrified others, was now terrified with this dream. Something about this dream made him afraid. This time however, the king remembered the dream and told it first to his magicians and sootsayers, but they of course could not interpret, though they heard the dream. For the second time, the king needed answers, and among his wise men, only Daniel was qualified to interpret the king's dream (*Daniel* 4: 10-17).

I fell asleep in my palace and dreamed I saw a tree standing in the middle of the earth. It was the tallest tree I had ever seen. [11] It grew bigger and stronger until its top seemed to touch heaven itself. Everyone in the world could see it.

[12] Its leaves were beautiful and it was loaded with fruit, enough to feed everyone

The animals of the field came to rest in its shade, and the birds happily built their nests in its branches. It provided rest and protection for all living things.

[13]Then in my dream as I lay in my bed, I saw a Watcher a Holy One come down from heaven, and say loudly to those with Him. "Cut this tree down. Strip it of its leaves cut off its branches and scatter its fruit. Drive away the animals that were under it, and also the bird that built their nests there. [15] But leave the stump and root in the ground. Put a band of iron and bronze around it and leave it alone. Leave it in the middle of the field, and let it get wet the morning dew. Let the man whom this tree represents live with the animals, and eat the grass of the field. [16]Take away his reason and give him the mind of an animal. Let seven times, that is, seven years pass by. [17] This was decided by the Holy One and those with Him so that all people will know that the Most High God who rules the universe also keeps a watchful eye on human affairs, He gives the various kingdoms to whomever He wills and sets over them the lowest of men.

Daniel to the Rescue

Daniel received the interpretation of the dream, but could not speak for a while because the meaning terrified him. He could not gather the courage to speak to the king, because of the prediction for his future. He sat in silence for one hour, for he was not sure, how to divulge the matter to the king, so as not to infuriate him. The king must have realized the difficulty he was experiencing to say the meaning, so he told Daniel not to make the dream or the interpretation trouble him. Daniel told the king, he wished the dream was not meant for him. The dream was about a very tall tree in the middle of the earth.

A tree in the middle of the earth represented the reign of Nebuchadnezzar, because Babylon occupied middle position of the then known world. The tree reached unto heaven, and the leaves were fair. Babylon was glorious and fruitful, and there was enough food for everyone.

Nebuchadnezzar's protection and support for all his subjects were represented by the beasts of the field that found shade under the tree, and the birds that rested in the branches. The tree was cut down leaving the stump, around which a band of iron and brass should be placed for its protection against decay. This meant the chance for future growth and greatness were preserved. "Let seven times pass over him", was the number of years he should be among the beasts in the field.

The day is coming when the wicked shall be cut down, and unlike Nebuchadnezzar, there will be nothing left, no hope of recovery. The fury of God will not be mingled with His mercy. They shall be destroyed root and branch. The dream and interpretations tell us that God is merciful and kind to humankind and that heaven takes interest in all the affairs of men. He sees more than we can ever hope to see with our mortal eyes. God knows our thoughts and intentions.

Heavenly beings cheerfully carry out the decree for the correction of evil. Man should know that he is not the one in charge of his fortune; God gives the power to get wealth and to become leaders. There is "One" who rules in the kingdom of men on whom humankind should depend. A successful leader should not be proud, for unless the Lord permits him/her to rule he/she cannot reach the position of honor. Nebuchadnezzar had to learn the hard way to be humble. Exaltation brings humility, but humility, will result in exaltation.

Though Daniel counseled with the king, he did not denounce him. He used kindness and persuasion, a lesson in time for anyone who may have the unenvied task to face an arrogant leader. He said, "Let my counsel be acceptable unto thee." Paul in *Hebrews* 13: 22 begs men to use words of exhortation.

If the king had heeded the counsel of Daniel, he might have averted the judgment God intended to meet out to him. His heart was filled with pride even twelve months after he received the warning from the interpretation of the dream.

He soon forgot the source of his strength. As he strut about his palace he saw the beauty and splendor of his kingdom he exclaimed! "Is not this great Babylon that I have built for the house of the kingdom by the might of my power, and for the honor of my majesty?" (*Daniel* 4:30).

Time had come for Nebuchadnezzar's humiliation. A voice from heaven announced the judgment and immediately, divine power executed it. His reason left him, and he left the palace and joined the beasts in the field. For seven years he was wet with the dew of heaven, miraculously however, he was unharmed all these years. God protected him because He is a forgiving and merciful God. He is not willing that any should perish but that all should come to a knowledge of the truth and repent. That is exactly what happened to Nebuchadnezzar.

> And at the end of the days, I Nebuchadnezzar, lifted up mine eyes unto heaven, and mine understanding returned unto me, and I blessed the Most High, and I praised and honored Him that lives forever, whose dominion is an everlasting dominion, and His kingdom is from generation to generation (*Daniel* 4:34) emphasis added.

David in *Psalm* 121: 1 admonishes humankind to lift up his eyes to the hills. Help comes from the Maker of heaven and earth. He is more willing to help us than we are willing to ask, so ask. Fall on the Rock now, and be broken of pride, arrogance, self-sufficiency, and worldliness. Jesus will, and can put the pieces of broken lives together again.

Though Nebuchadnezzar, showed arrogance and pride as the monarch of Babylon. God looked at his heart and saw honesty of heart, purity of purpose and integrity, which He could use to glorify His name. He does not see as man sees. He looks beyond our faults and sees our needs. Though others may cast us away as worthless stones, God is willing to work with us, to recover the gem-hidden way below the surface.

He knows how to break, reshape sand and polish the battered and broken for His use. The proud king symbolized as the head of gold, died a believer in the God of heaven. Who would have thought that a man who was willing to sacrifice the lives of three innocent young men who dared disobey him, could be a chosen vessel in the cause of God. Pray for rulers, kings, presidents, prime ministers, and chiefs.

[15]   *Daniel & the Revelation* pp. 67, 68.

CHAPTER 13

Out With the Gold in With the Silver

After the death of Nebuchadnezzar, about four kings occupied the throne over a period of several years, last of who was his grandson Belshazzar. Only two years after the death of Nebuchadnezzar, there was war between the Babylonian kingdoms, and the Medes and Persians. The latter triumphed over the Babylonians for years. However, Babylon the only city in the East held out and never succumbed to the attack of the Medes and Persians.

The relative success against the Medes and Persians was to be celebrated. The Babylonians comforted themselves about the security of Babylon and gave little thought to would-be invasions. They felt very safe and unreachable. The impregnable walls of the city were sources of comfort. There was enough food to last the population many years. They had skilful and well-trained soldiers, and the Euphrates River that ran through the city, provided added security against intruders and would-be invaders. It is little wonder that Belshazzar, now in the third year of his reign felt very secure and comfortable within the walls of Babylon. He and his men sneered at Cyrus and his men for uselessly trying to get within the walls. Belshazzar had no idea that he was about to face a stupendous event in his life from which he would not recover.

Similar to the false hope and confidence displayed in the invincible, unsinkable Titanic, Belshazzar thought fabricated devices were a guarantee for safety. While he and his lords, wives and concubines, and all others within the city were drinking and reveling, little attention was paid to details for safety. The drunken guards left the gates to the city opened and unattended. At the same time, the Persians were working feverishly to re-channel the Euphrates River to make entry into the city through the riverbed.

The Babylonian empire soon collapsed. The king's elaborate feast came to an abrupt end. His excessive drinking greatly altered his sense of reason to the extent that he even drank wine from the sacred vessels from the temple. While they celebrated their gods' superior power over Jehovah, there was silence, as a hand was writing his fate on the wall, over against the plaster. The party was interrupted with deadly silence, and in the meantime, the Persians were fast closing in on them.

In *Daniel* 5:5 we read, "In the same hour came forth fingers of a man's hand, and wrote over against the candlestick upon the plaster of the wall of the king's palace: and the king saw the part of the hand that wrote." His immediate emotion was fear. He was terrified and his knees trembled. He had absolutely no control over what was happening to him, and even if he wanted to disguise the fact that he was afraid, his knees, and countenance would not allow him. He forgot his boasting, dignity and revelry, and he called for his soothsayers and astrologers to interpret the mysterious writing, but they could not.

Daniel again came to the palace to interpret what the wise men of Babylon could not solve. He graciously but categorically refused the gifts promised to him by the king. This unplanned visit was for the terrified Belshazzar. The first question he asked was if Daniel came from the captivity of Judah. Belshazzar still did not acknowledge that these Hebrew men, including Daniel, were servants of the Living God and no one can hold God's children captive except God wills it.

Though he saw Daniel as a "captive," he looked to him to do a task that his "free" men could not do. He even promised Daniel gifts, but Daniel said, "Let thy rewards be to another." Daniel wished to separate himself from the gift-seeking soothsayers of Babylon.

Daniel rehearsed the experience of his grandfather Nebuchadnezzar, and told Belshazzar that although he knew all that happened to Nebuchadnezzar, he did not humble himself; instead, he lifted up himself against the God of heaven. He went so far as to use the sacred vessels of God to praise the senseless gods of men's inventions. He told him that the hand had been sent from God, whom he had insultingly challenged. He then proceeded to explain the writing.

Verse 25 And this is the writing that was written, "MENE, MENE, TEKEL, UPHARSIN."

This is the interpretation

26 MENE-God has numbered thy kingdom and finished it.

27 TEKEL: Thou art weighed in the balances, and art found wanting.

28 PERES; Thy kingdom is divided and given to the Medes and Persians.

Note, while all this was taking place the Medes and Persians were making progress to enter the city. They rechanneled the Euphrates River, entered the riverbed and gained access through the unguarded gates left unattended by the drunken guards. This was supposed to be one of their strong defenses, now used as an effective tool against them. With drawn swords, the Persians entered the palace of the king and surprised him.

A famous song-writer says, "The arm of flesh will fail you." Security outside of Christ is, false security, and failure is inevitable. That night Belshazzar was called to reckoning but was found wanting. The reign of the head of gold ended that night. Belshazzar was killed and the empire of

Babylon was history, because the empire collapsed the same night. This is a warning to all who disobey the, "Thus says the Lord" and follow their own inclinations. The judgment of God may not be swift or dramatic, but a day of reckoning is coming when God is going to bring the nations of earth before Him to give an account of their stewardship.

Note there are but two forces in the world, "good" and "evil". There is no middle ground; we are obeying one or the other. We are either spiritual or carnal. If we obey God we are spiritual, if we disobey Him we are carnal, and the word of God says, the carnal mind is enmity against God. "Because the carnal mind is enmity against God: for it is not subject to the law of God, neither indeed can be" *(Romans* 8: 7). After all God has done for man, it would be wise to surrender the will to Him, so He can use us for His service.

The stage was now set for the **second** kingdom foretold by the interpretation of the image of Nebuchadnezzar, the breast and arms of silver, the Medes Persians.

> "That night they slew him on his father's throne. The deed unnoticed the hand unknown: Crownless and scepter less Belshazzar lay, A robe of purple round a form of clay."

(Edwin Arnold," *The Feast of Belshazzar*," Poetical Works, p. 170.) *(Daniel & the Revelation* p.82).

The Medes and Persians

Darius the Persian ascended to the throne of Babylon, in **538 B.C.** Two years later, he died and Cyrus took the throne. During this time, Daniel continued to be an influential person in Babylon. With the victories of Cambyses and Darius Hystaspes, the provinces of Babylon grew in number to one hundred seventy. Over every prince for each of these provinces, were three presidents, chief of who was Daniel.

Darius could have felt threatened by this influential person and could demote or banish him, but he was discerning and wise. He thought not only to use Daniel, but also to promote him to that coveted office. There is no doubt that the reason he recognized Daniel, was due to his integrity and fidelity. Daniel had an excellent spirit.

The jealousy of the other rulers sought to discredit him, but Daniel was faithful and true to the law of God. They could find no occasion to condemn him except concerning obedience to God, so they used his faithfulness to God and plotted against him.

Dear reader who profess to be a child of God, can it be said of you that an "excellent spirit is in you?" Daniel experienced, many difficult times, yet he overcame. We can take courage from his actions and be faithful. Daniel experienced many challenges but he never gave in. He went to Babylon as a captive, and time did not erase that fact, for even when he was called to interpret dreams his counterparts could not do, he was referred to as the captive of Judah. He was one of four among a nation, who made his spiritual presence felt. Evil practices of idolatry surrounded him; he was among this evil behavior, which was the worst sin of the day. All these people knew was sorcery, divination, and idolatry.

Earlier we read that Daniel "purposed" in his heart. To be an overcomer, we too should make deliberate efforts to obey God rather than man. Be intentional about choosing wisely. Doing the right and living honest lives may not be easy, but the results will be rewarding. Be aware though, that suffering, hardships and trials, may come before success. Daniel was a captive, and a prisoner of war, condemned to die, but later became prime minister of Babylon. Joseph spent years as a servant or in prison, before becoming prime minister of Egypt. Moses the Egyptian general spent forty years in the wilderness, tending sheep, before becoming the leader of the Exodus. David spent years as a fugitive, before becoming king over Israel.

Be willing to carry the cross before you wear the crown. Winning is not so much about how you start, but how you finish. Many who have started strong have fallen by the way, while some who have started out falling and failing have endured to the end.

CHAPTER 14

The Plot Against Daniel

Some of Daniel's nefarious, scheming co-workers, approached the king with flattering words of their loyalty and dedication for him. The unsuspecting king signed the letter, which stated that, no prayer or petition should be made to any man or god except to the king for thirty days. The petition seemed general and reasonable, because no mention was made of the God of the Hebrews. If they had so done the king would have suspected their plans, and not sign the decree.

Daniel realized that they hatched a plot against him, but he did nothing to stop the process. Instead, he continued his faithfulness to God and left the plan to His Divine will. He did not leave the capital to pretend to be gone on business, so he would not be seen praying. Instead, he continued to pray three times a day with his face towards Jerusalem, as was his custom.

The men pretending to do business came and saw him praying. Immediately they hastened to report the matter to the king. They described him as, "That Daniel, which is of the children of the captivity of Judah, regards thee not O king, nor the decree that thou hast signed" *(Daniel*

6:13). The king then realized the plan was a trap to condemn Daniel, his faithful and trusted servant. Though, he tried long and hard to undo the damage in order to save Daniel, it was of no avail, because the laws of the Medes and Persians were unalterable.

They threw Daniel into the den of hungry lions, where he remained all night. He did not suffer any harm at all, because God had sent His angels and shut the lions' mouths so they could not hurt him. The king's all night fasting, because of what had happened to Daniel, showed his genuine interest in Daniel. He condemned himself for having a part in the matter.

Early the next morning, at the first sign of dawn, the king dressed and hurried to the lions' den because he wondered if Daniel's God had been able to protect him. As the king approached he called Daniel, with a lamentable voice, "O Daniel servant of the living God, is thy God able to deliver thee?"(*Daniel* 6:20). The king asked a revealing question as to where his mind was, not on the Chaldeans, not the magicians but the God Daniel served. Daniel lived in a real world among people who were envious of right doing, just as is the case today, but can our friends, relatives, coworkers and bosses experience the power of the God we serve?

> It may be a difficult matter for men in high position to pursue the path of undeviating integrity whether they shall receive praise or censure. Yet this is the only safe course. All the rewards which they might gain by selling their honor would be only as the breath from polluted lips, as dross to be consumed in the fire. [16]

Daniel had every reason to be angry with the king for allowing him to be in the den, but he was not angry. Here again is a lesson, for the professed servants of the Living God. Instead of doing as Daniel did, we maximize the minor and forget the bigger picture, often losing favorable opportunities to witness for God. May the experience of Daniel be etched in the minds of every reader and help us to be people of integrity. Daniel responded with utter respect to the call of the king and let him know who was responsible for his deliverance.

21 Then said Daniel unto the king, O king live forever

22 My God hath sent His angels and hath shut the lions mouths, that they have not hurt me: for as much as before Him, innocency was found in me: and also before thee, O king, have I done no hurt.

23 Then was the king exceeding glad for him and commanded, that they should take Daniel up out of the den. So Daniel was taken up out of the den, and no manner of hurt was found upon him, because he believed in his God *(Daniel 6: 21-23).*

Daniel was preserved by the power of God, so he suffered no hurt. That is what faith in God can do. One songwriter says, If we did not have trials, we would not know what faith in God can do. Friends when our ways please the Lord, He will make a way where there is no way. He has done it for Daniel and the other believers; He will do it for us too.

Those who sought Daniel's life suffered their fate with the hungry lions. Daniel did not ask for revenge, it was the king who ordered the execution of the men who plotted against him. The same lions meant for Daniel were the same ones that killed the men. God will fight our battles. "The Lord shall fight for you and ye shall hold your peace" *(Exodus 14: 14).*

"The reason that just a few of you can chase and defeat a thousand is because of the Lord, not because of your strength. It's the Lord who's fighting for you" *(Joshua 23: 10,* CW).

God Honors Fidelity

God defends His faithful children. He knows our hearts and answers the prayers of rich and poor alike. Whenever the "lions" of our circumstances face us, He tells us to call on Him and He will hear and save us from impending danger.

Isaiah 41:10 says "So don't be afraid. I am with you. Do not be dismayed, for I am Your God. I will strengthen you. I will help you. I will hold you up with the right hand of my righteousness."

"Where are those among you who will reverence the Lord and obey His Servant? If there are such let them put their faith in the Lord" . . . (*Isaiah 50: 10 CW*).

We do not have to fear the enemy in any form, because God tells us not to fear, we need to put our trust in Him when problems, or tensions assail us. Many years ago, a classmate and I went ingathering. We went to a few houses in a particular neighborhood, and decided to ascend the hill to another house. The house was barely visible from the foot of the hill; therefore, we had to start climbing before we could call to alert the householder that visitors were on the way. We had no idea what to expect, but we were working for the Lord, so acting on the faith prayer we had made earlier, we kept going, up, up.

As we came nearer to the house, we began to call, to alert the residents that someone was approaching. Instead of a friendly voice to greet us, it was the thunderous noise of two or three huge barking dogs, bounding towards us. There was no escape, and the feint call of a child running towards us drowned in the loud barks of the approaching dogs. Soon an adult came running and calling for the dogs. It was too late I froze, and stopped dead in my tracks. By now, my friend had hurried towards the child, who guided her towards the house. I was to face the angry dogs alone, or so I thought. Very quickly, I sent up a prayer, and as quickly as they rushed towards me, they stopped in their tracks.

It was a miracle I was not hurt. The homeowner was able to control them and hurried them back to the house. Too shaken to finish the journey, I remained where I was until my friend returned. God answered my prayer instantly. He did it for Daniel, and He will do it for you, for similar or different circumstances. We must however remember that God will sometimes allow things to happen for our greater good and for His honor. Whatever He chooses, His way is always the best way. God saved the Hebrew men from the burning fiery furnace, and He will deliver us from our furnaces too. We do not need to lose heart nor lower our standards to please any one; we should rather honor the God of heaven.

[16] S. D. A. *Bible Commentary* Vol., 4, p.1171.

CHAPTER 15

Animals of Significance

In Daniel chapter 2 king Nebuchadnezzar had a dream about an image, whose prophetic interpretation, meant kingdoms from his time to the end of time. Similarly, Daniel had a dream in which he saw four beasts, each of which represented the same period as the head, breast, thigh, legs, feet and toes of the image of *Daniel 2*.

The first vision came at night, while I was in bed.

I saw an ocean being whipped up by mighty winds coming from all directions. Then four huge animals came up out of the stormy sea, one after another, each one different (*Daniel* 7:2, 3 CW).

The first three animals were familiar, but the fourth was a dreadful nondescript animal. It was very strong and had iron teeth and ten horns. After a while three of the horns were destroyed and a little one which had eyes like that of a man, and a mouth that spoke great things replaced them. The animals he saw were as follows:

The **first** was like a **lion** and had eagle's wings: with the wings plucked and it stood on his feet as if a man, and it had a man's heart.

The **second** was like a **bear**, which raised its self on one side. It had three ribs in its mouth, and was told to get up and eat much flesh.

The **third** was like a **leopard,** which had four wings like a fowl. It had four heads and was very powerful.

The **fourth** was dreadful, terrible, and **different** from the other beasts. It was very strong, and had iron teeth, which broke in pieces and devoured and crushed the residue under its feet. It had ten horns, three of which were pulled out, and one little horn, came up in place of them. This little horn had eyes like a man, and a mouth that spoke great things (*Daniel* 7:4-8).

Beasts out of the sea
www.Goodsalt.com

First kingdom—Babylon (Lion)

Like the image of Daniel 2, the first kingdom was Babylon ruled by Nebuchadnezzar. The first beast of Daniel was a lion, which had eagle's wings. *Habakkuk* 1: 6-8 describe the Chaldeans being able to, "fly as eagle and hasteth to eat." Babylon during Nebuchadnezzar's reign was strong and its conquests were rapid. However, the lion lost its wings after a time, and it was not as bold as a lion. It now had a man's heart, weak and faint. Hence, Babylon as history records became weak and effeminate through the indulgence of wealth and luxury.

Second Kingdom—Medo-Persia (Bear)

As was mentioned in the prophecy of Daniel each succeeding kingdom would be weaker than its predecessor was. Hence, the next kingdom, the second, was a bear representing Medo-Persia. This second kingdom was inferior to the lion just as how Medo-Persia the chest and arms of silver was inferior to Babylon, the head of gold, as depicted by the image of Daniel 2.

The bear represented two nationalities, the Medes and the Persians. It raised itself up on one side. This is also mentioned in Daniel 8, as the two horns, one being higher than the other, the higher coming up last. This is the raising itself on one side. The Medes and Persians oppressed the three provinces of **Babylon**, **Lydia**, and **Egypt**, portrayed by the three ribs in the mouth of the bear. The character of a bear was well represented by the habit of a bear. They are cruel and rapacious. This behavior exemplified what the bear should do, "Arise devour much flesh." The overthrow of these provinces are proof of their wickedness. After the fall of Belshazzar, they continued to rule for a period of two hundred and seven years (207) to the year **331 B.C.** (*Daniel & the Revelation* p.94).

Third kingdom—Greece (Leopard)

The third kingdom was Greece represented by a leopard, which would be the same as the belly and thigh of the image of Daniel 2. This leopard had four wings, which denote incredible swiftness, much faster than the lion, the first beast. This swift animal was Alexander the great. His military accomplishments were unmatched by the best of his time.

He was master in the combination of various arms, which won him great admiration. Among his strengths, were his ability to campaign effectively in winter, he was a great organizer, and he executed well. In ten years, he had only two serious political problems.

Though he had good political strategies and was very successful at what he did, he had a serious personal problem, he was a drunkard, which was his demise. At the early age of thirty-one, he died of a fever brought about by a drunken stupor.

He conquered the world but could not conquer his own world of bad habit. The swiftness of the bear that represented his reign, also spoke to his swift early death. Alexander's infant sons were murdered, so after his death, his four generals received portions of the divided kingdom.

Fourth kingdom—Rome (Terrible nondescript animal)

This beast had four heads.
- Cassander had Macedonia and Greece in the west.
- Lysimachus had Thrace and the parts of Asia on the Hellespont and the Bosphorus on the north.
- Ptolemy had Egypt, Lydia Arabia, Palestine, and Coele Syria in the south.
- Seleuctus had Syria and all the rest of Alexander's dominion in the east.

(*Daniel & the Revelation* p. 95).

Thus, the four heads of the leopard denoted these four divisions after the death of Alexander. The fourth beast was dreadful and terrible. This corresponds to the fourth division of the beast of *Daniel* 2 which were the legs of iron. Rome's actions befit this beast which was terrible and excel in strength. It devoured with its iron teeth, broke in pieces all who stood against it. It ground the nations under its feet. Its ten horns as described by *Daniel* 7: 24 are ten kings or kingdoms which should arise out of this empire.

In **A.D. 70**, Pagan Rome destroyed the temple in Jerusalem and ended the temple services as described by *Daniel* 8: 9-13. However, according to verse 14, the prophecy was to extend close to eighteen century beyond **A.D. 70**. This means that the little horn is both **pagan** and **papal Rome** (Treasures of life p. 89). (For the relationship between pagan and papal Rome see *Daniel* 7). Daniel saw the little horn as a persecuting power. *Daniel* 7:26 says "The judgment shall sit, and they shall take away his dominion, to consume and to destroy it unto the end." Look back on *Daniel* 7 and notice some events that occurred in this prophecy (*Bible Readings* p.89).

- The division of the fourth, symbolized by the ten horns. The little horn was both **pagan** and **papal** Rome.
- The establishment of the papacy, (symbolized by the little horn, before which three horns fell).

Concerning the "little horn," depicted as the great antichrist power of history, there are **nine** characteristics that identify and classify the little horn.

1   Geographically, it originates in Western Europe because it came up among the **ten** kingdoms mentioned earlier (*Daniel* 7:7).
2   It came up after the **ten kingdoms,** took the place of three of the uprooted kingdoms, therefore, it came after **476 B.C** (*Daniel* 7:7).

3   It uprooted three of the ten tribes as it came to power.

4   Had eyes like a man and a mouth speaking great things (*verse* 8) which indicates that a human being would be at the head of this power, represented by the little horn (*Daniel* 7:20).

5   Different from the first horns (*verse* 24) which means it would be a different kind of power from those political kingdoms, which preceded it.

6   Speaks great words against the Most High. (*verse* 25) Speaks great things and blasphemies. (*Revelation* 13:5) *John* 10:30-33 blasphemy means, "He makes Himself God." In *Mark* 2: 7, blasphemy means, claiming to be able to forgive sins.

7   Wears out the saints of the Most High—A persecuting power, who makes war with God's people, and causes them to be put to death (*Daniel* 7:7).

8   Will think to change times and laws. The attempt was made, but failed, because the moral law of God is unchangeable (*Daniel* 7:25).

9   Time allotted will be until time and times and the dividing of times or 1260 years (See Appendix B and *Daniel* 12: 7) (*Daniel* 7:25).

An Exact Fulfillment

There is but one power in history, that befits the little horn power mentioned in *Daniel* 7, and that is the Catholic Church. Consider these events in history as proof.

First

The papacy arose in Western Europe, at the very heart of the Pagan Roman Empire in Rome itself.

Second

It came up after **476 A.D.** In the year **538 A.D., Emperor Justinian's,** decree to assign absolute pre-eminence to the Church of Rome, went into effect. This is history (see chapter 18).

Third

When the papacy arose, it was opposed by three of the tribes, which had taken over at the collapse of the Roman Empire. The Vandals, Ostrogoths, and Heruli, were Arian powers who were in strong opposition to the rise of the Catholic Church. As it will be discovered later in this study, Rome will destroy any force, organization, or nation that opposes her. This erratic and demoralizing behavior of Rome was brought to bear on these three opposing tribes. The armies of Rome uprooted and extirpated these tribes. The last of the three was destroyed in **538 A. D.** (above paragraph) when Justinian's decree went into effect.

Fourth

A man was at the head of the Catholic System. When the horn of the he goat was broken, four little ones replaced it, and out of one of them came up a little horn with eyes like a man and a mouth speaking great things *(Daniel* 8:8, 9).

Fifth

The papacy was a different kind of power from the other political kingdoms before it. It was a religio-political system, quite different from anything seen in the world before. Religion and politics were amalgamated *(Daniel & the Revelation p.297)*.

Sixth

It is a power that speaks great words and blasphemy against the Most High. *Daniel 7: 25*, (first part) speaks to this exactly. The Catholic Church claims to have power to forgive sins. *F. Lucil Ferraris* says, "The pope is of so great dignity and so exalted, that he is not a mere man, but as he were God, and the Vicar of God" *(Daniel & the Revelation p.113)*. Thus, the papacy meets the identity of the little horn power.

Seventh

Any religious system that opposed the Catholic Church was generally severely punished. In the middle Ages, millions of people were tortured and killed by the Catholic inquisitions. When confronted by heresy . . . she recourses to force, corporal punishment, torture. She creates tribunals like the inquisition. She calls the laws of the state to its aid. This is especially true of their actions in the **16th Century** in regards to Protestants in France under Francis 1, and in England under Mary Tudor, who tortured the heretics *(Treasures of life p.119)*.

Eighth v. 25

The little horn power would think to change times and God's laws. The Catholic Church in one of its presumptuous attempts to tamper with God's laws has removed the second commandment from her doctrinal books and catechism, because it condemns the worship of idols (images). They have divided the tenth commandment in two to make up the total of ten. In this way, they have thought to change God's times and laws.

Ninth

The duration of the papal power would be for **1260** years. The papacy started in **538 A.D.** and ended in **1798**, when the French general Berthier marched his army into Rome and carried away the Pope as prisoner, where he died. They also confiscated all the properties of the church. The French directory government decreed that there would never be another Bishop of Rome. As far as the world was concerned and by all outward appearances the Catholic church was dead, because of the period of quiet after the pope's arrest. She lost control after exactly **1260** years. This loss however, was temporary because in *Revelation* 13: 3, the Bible says his deadly wound would heal. "And I saw one of his heads as it were wounded to death; and his deadly wound was healed: and all the world wondered after the beast." All these evidences and more, identify the papacy, the Roman Catholic Church as the little horn.

Matthew 24 speaks to the time of trouble just before Jesus comes. History will repeat itself, and the persecution meted out to followers of Christ in the dark ages will be implemented, only more intensely. Believers in Christ need not be afraid for Jesus promised to hide His children in time of trouble. Verse 22 says He will also shorten those days, for the elect sake.

CHAPTER 16

The Beast

Revelation 13 and *Daniel* 7 describe the beast as a strange animal with a body of a leopard, feet of a bear, and a head of a lion. His rule should continue for forty-two (**42**) months, which is equivalent to **1260** years. *Daniel* 7 refers to this as time and times and half a time, which is the same as 31/2 prophetic years or (**1260** years). Power was given him to make war with the saints. Note that the beast of Revelation is the same power as the little horn in Daniel. Both accounts are symbolic of the papacy. This is God's graphic illustration of the papal power represented by the little horn power as it came up to exercise authority over the earth for **1260** years.

The Little Horn

Daniel 7: 24 says, "He shall be diverse from the first, and he shall subdue three kings." The Papacy,

> This power supports a union of church and state, the church having the greater dominance.

which arose on the ruins of the Roman Empire, differed from all previous forms of Roman power in that it was an ecclesiastical despotism, claiming universal dominion over both spiritual and temporal affairs, especially the former. It was a union of church and state, frequently with the church the dominant. The Pope calls himself "King" and "Pontifex Maximus," is Caesar's successor. [17]

> In *Daniel 7: 21* the little horn made war with the saints, and prevailed against them. This notable horn, which was Alexander the Great, was the first king of the Macedonian Empire. He denotes as the he goat (Dan. 8:5), that attacked the ram, Medo Persia. The battles between the Greeks and the Persians were very fierce. History records some of these scenes, which clearly support the prophecy—'a ram standing before the river and the goat running towards him in, "the fury of his power."

Does the Bible have anything to say about presumption of the head of this power? Sure it does. 2 *Thessalonians* 2: 4 "He will exalt himself by opposing all who truly worship God. He will set himself up in the midst of the church and speak for God as if he were God" (CW). The following are extracts mostly from Roman Catholic writers; to the extent, the Papacy has done this. Ponder for a while.

In 1929, Cardinal Gasparri met Premier Mussolini, to settle a long time dispute and the Pope restored temporal power to the Papacy, thus healing a wound of 59 years (*Bible Reading* p. 114). At this time, the Pope became king once more and the Vatican was recognized as

Sun worship first started as a pagan system of religion filled with immoralities and blasphemous idolatry . . .

the political sovereign power. Since that date to this, the strength of the Papacy has been advancing tremendously. (See Appendix C).

To this historic event, the San Francisco Chronicle of February 12, 1929, carried the pictures of the men signing the Concordat. The affixed caption read, "Heal Wound of Many Years." Inadvertently the Newspaper carried the very words mentioned in prophecy, "Heal" and "Wound."

Most countries of the world have sent political representatives to the Vatican City. The views and instructions of the Pope are heard around the world and millions look to the papal power as the greatest influence in political and religious mattes. The wound has been healed, and the world is wondering after the beast.

The Pope makes several trips around the world trying to bring peace. Everywhere he goes, thousands of people flock to hear and see him, and they revere him. It therefore means whenever he recommends laws (as they are now making) for unity among religions, church and state, many will not question his integrity, but will agree and comply. Suffice it to say, nothing is wrong in honoring this person who is trying to do good, but he should be considered a man like any other man, for so is he. One day we "ALL," shall face the Judge, Jesus Himself to give an account of our deeds. There will be no exemption regardless of present status. Paul advises that no one should think of himself more highly than he ought to think (*Romans* 12:3).

With the need for families to have quality family time and with the suggestion of a recommend day of worship as a means of accomplishing this goal of having better families, many will agree without giving the matter second thought. Rome is now working through the ecumenical system to control the world, or to occupy Center Stage to attract allegiance to a system not sanctioned by God. By the very definition of the words ecumenical and catholic, the work of this body holds true.

Ecumenical means inhabited world, and catholic means worldwide; hence, this global movement is busy trying to unite people to a body, which believes in a doctrinal formation. The Catholic Doctrinal Formation upholds sacred **scripture and sacred tradition** as their rule of faith, which means their belief in tradition is the same as their belief in scripture. Friends do not allow tradition to take center stage over the Bible. On the other hand, the Protestant Doctrinal Formation is **Sola Scriptura,** the Bible and **the Bible only.** For Protestants the Bible is the source of doctrine and belief. The Bible occupies Center Stage in their rule of faith.

In Philip Schaff *Creed of Christendom* (*New* York: Charles Schribner's Sons), vole 2, p. 262, *(Pastor Aeterrnus)* published the following in the fourth session of the Vatican Council 1870), chap. 3.

> We teach and define that it is a dogma divinely revealed: that the Roman Pontiff, when he speaks excathedra, that is when in discharge of the office of pastor and doctor of all Christians, by virtue of his supreme Apostolic authority, he defines a doctrine regarding faith or morals to be held by the universal Church by the divine assistance promised to him in blessed Peter, is possessed of that infallibility with which the divine Redeemer willed that His church be endowed for defining doctrine regarding faith or morals: and that therefore such definitions of the Roman Pontiff are irreformable of themselves, and not from the consent of the church *(Ibid. chap. 4, pp. 269, 270).*

Be aware! Study the word for yourself, only God is infallible. All men are created equal. All of us are accountable to God. No one has the right to legislate a day of worship. We are free moral beings, with the power of choice. Do not be taken off guard to believe or adhere to any belief system that is based on any belief but the Bible only. "Choose you this day whom ye will serve" . . . *(Joshua* 24:15).

Here too are portions of twenty-seven propositions known as the "Dictates of Hilderbrand," under the name George V11, being Pope from (1073-1087)

- That the Roman Pontiff alone is justly styled universal.
- That no person . . . may live under the same roof with one excommunicated by the Pope.
- That all princes should kiss his feet.
- That it is lawful for him to depose emperors.
- That his sentence is not to be reviewed by any one: while he alone can review the decisions of others.
- That he can be judged by no one.
- That the Roman Church never erred, nor will it, according to the Scriptures ever err.
- That no one is to be accounted a Catholic who does not harmonize with the Roman Church.
- That he can absolve subjects from their allegiance to unrighteous rulers.—Cesare Baronius, Annales, year 1076, sec, 31-33, vol. 17 (1869 ed.) pp. 405, 406, translated (*Bible Readings* p. 83).

The Dragon and Sun Worship

The city of Babylon was the first city of the dragon on the earth. Sun worship first started as a pagan system of religion, filled with immoralities and blasphemous idolatry, with licentious ceremonies and degrading rites. What started as a practice of worship among the Babylonians, continued with the succeeding kingdom of Medo-Persia. During their rule, Baal worship continued to be the major form of worship.

The Seed of the Dragon

The seed of the dragon appeared in the form of the beast of *Revelation* 13. It is part leopard with feet of a bear, and mouth of a lion. This animal came up out of the sea and had seven heads and ten horns each horn with a crown. (cf. *Daniel* 7). The dragon empowered him by giving him his power, seat and great authority. (*Revelation* 13:1-3). It drew most of its strength from pagan Rome.

"And the beast which I saw was like unto a leopard, and his feet, were as the feet of a bear and his mouth, as the mouth of a lion: and the dragon gave him his power and his seat and great authority" (*Revelation* 13: 2).

In **330 A.D.**, Constantine turned the whole city of Rome over to the Pope as the seat of his authority. The removal of the capital of the empire of Rome to Constantinople left the western church without imperial power and so it was free to develop its own form of organization. "The Bishop of Rome was now the greatest man in the west and was soon forced to become the political and spiritual leader" (*The Rise of the Medieval Church p.* 168).

The power of Rome tried to stamp out the truth by violence but could not, so strategy and deception were introduced. Rome organized its own counterfeit religious system and brought in pagan doctrines and philosophies from the old empires of Babylon, Medo Persia, Greece and pagan Rome, and combined them with Christian teachings. All four kingdoms afore mentioned, with their religio-political systems, tried to destroy God's principles by substitution, and counterfeit, but were unsuccessful. Nevertheless, counterfeit doctrines crept into worship. Pagan idols were left at the door of the temple, but those of Peter, Mary, and other saints were inside the temple. Thus, Satan attempted to destroy millions through deception.

The following pagan ideas form part of the church, deliberately replacing the true form of worship in accordance with the word of God:

- *Tradition* instead of the word of God.
- *Sprinkling* instead of baptism.
- *The pope* instead of the Holy Spirit.
- *Transubstantiation* instead of communion.
- *The changed law* instead of the eternal law of God.
- *Taxes, indulgencies* instead of tithe.
- *Purgatory* instead of death.
- *The mark of the beast* instead of the Seal of God. (*Treasures of Life*, pp. 601-603).

Take a moment to assimilate the above, and consider if you believe or practice any of these traditions. Then you have a responsibility to turn away. May God give you the courage.

The mark of the beast is always opposed to the Seal of God (*Revelation* 2, 3; 14: 9, 10). My friend half-truth is error. It is not possible to profess to love the Lord, and engage in idol worship. Actions should agree with belief. Do not let the deception of Satan's counterfeit fool you. Believe and practice Biblically sound doctrine.

No person has the right to dictate to the conscience a style of worship that cannot stand the test of the Bible. "Study to show yourself approved unto God." Anyone who honors the traditions of men over obedience to the word of God worships God in vain. "But in vain do they worship me, teaching for doctrines the commandments of men" (*Matthew* 15:9).

Daniel 7: 25 reveals the things the little horn would do:

- He shall speak great words against the Most High
- Shall wear out the saints of the Most High
- Think to change times and laws.

This he would do for time and times, and half a time, or three and a half years, which is **1260** days, or years which lasted to **1798**. The papacy was wounded, but his wound will be healed and it will return with great force. This power is gaining momentum and will repeat and use force to have people comply with its dictates. No one who cast away the law of God for tradition, or man's decisions, is honoring God. Exercise your right, follow conscience inspired by the Holy Spirit.

[17] Adolf Harnack, *What Is Christianity?* (New York: G. P. Putman's Sons, 1903), p.270

Bible Reading p. 82.

CHAPTER 17

The Pompous Little Horn

"And he shall speak great words against the Most High" (*Daniel* 7:25). The beast speaks in blasphemies against God and His tabernacles and those who dwell in heaven.

Little Horn to "Speak Great Words against the Most High"

The gospels of Luke and John cite two instances of blasphemy. In John 10:33 the Jews falsely accused Jesus of blasphemy because they said, "Thou art a man and makest Thyself God." Jesus was "Immanuel, God With Us." Jesus is truly God. However, for a man to assume the responsibilities of God, that is blasphemy.

In *Luke* 5:21 the Pharisees asked a question, "Who can forgive sins, but God alone?" Here again Jesus had the authority to pardon sins for He was/is divine. When mortal man claims such authority, it is without doubt blasphemy. "The priest holds the place of Savior Himself, when, he by saying 'Ego te absolvo' [I thee absolve], he absolves from sin . . . To pardon a single sin requires all the omnipotence of God . . . But what only God can do by His omnipotence, the priest can also do by saying, 'Ego te absolve a peccatistuis' . . . Innocent III has written 'Indeed, it is not too much to say that in view of the sublimity of their offices the priests are so many gods.'" [18]

My friend have you seen where a system headed by a man, (predicted in prophecy many years ago) is usurping the authority of God? With due respect to those who in ignorance, worship according to the dictates of man over the, thus saith the Lord, today if you hear His voice do not harden your heart, run to the Rock.

They further believe that when the priests utter the words, HOC EST CORPUS MEUM that means [This is My Body]—God himself descends on the altar and comes whenever they call Him. They place Him in their hands even though they should be his enemies. They claim they can move Him from place to place, as they will. They have total control over Him and can even shut him up in the tabernacle or carry Him outside. They can even decide to eat His flesh, or give His flesh to others to eat. "Oh how very great is their power," says Laurence Justinian, speaking of priests. "A word falls from their lips and the body of Christ is there substantially formed from the matter of bread, and the Incarnate Word descended is found really present on the table of the altar" *(Treasures of Life* 524).

"Thus the priest may, in certain manner, be called the creator of his Creator . . . 'The power of the priest,' says St. Bernardine of Sienna, 'is the power of the divine person; for the transubstantiation of the bread requires as much power as the creation of the world."[19]

This prophecy was fulfilled in the time of the pontiffs, many evidences show they have accepted titles, which belong to God alone. Lucius Ferrarias in his *Prompta Bibliotheca* refers to by the *Catholic Encyclopedia* as "variable encyclopedia of religious knowledge" and "a precious mine of information," says in the following articles on the pope.

"The pope is of such lofty and supreme dignity that, properly speaking he has not been established in any rank of dignity but rather has been placed upon the very summit of rank of dignities. The pope is called most holy because he is rightfully presumed to be such . . ." (*Treasures of Life*, p.114).

"The pope alone is deservedly called by the name 'most holy,' because he alone is the vicar of Christ, who is the fountain and source and fullness of all holiness . . . 'is like-wise the divine monarch and supreme emperor and king of kings.' . . . Hence, the pope is crowned with a triple a crown, as king of heaven and of earth and of the lower regions . . . For he is of so great dignity and power that he forms one and the same tribunal with Christ" . . . (*Ibid.*, p. 114).

> The pope is, as it were, God on earth, sole sovereign of the faithful of Christ, Chief king of kings, having plentitude of power, to whom has been entrusted by the omnipotent God direction not only of the earthly but also of the heavenly kingdom. The pope is called most holy because he is rightfully presumed to be such . . . The pope is of great authority and power that he can modify, explain, or interpret even divine laws. [20]

"He is not only a Priest forever, but also a King of kings and Lord of lords."—*La Civilta Cattolica*, March 18, 1871, quoted in Leonard Woolsey Bacon. An inside View of the Vatican Council (American Tract Society Ed.). p.229, n.

One of the leading doctrines of Romanism is that the pope is the visible head of the universal church of Christ. He is higher than all bishops and pastors, and has supreme authority over them. The pope has the titles of Deity, and is called, "Lord God the Pope" He is considered infallible (*Great Controversy* pp. 48, 595).

Christopher Marcellus, at the fourth session of the fifth Lateran Council in an oration to the Pope exclaimed, "Thou art the shepherd, thou art the physician, thou art the director, thou art the husbandman; finally, thou art another God on earth."

(P. Joannis Harduin, *Acia Conciliorum*, Vol. 1X, p. 1651 in *Daniel and the Revelation* p.114 and paragraph 4).

> Adam Clarke says on verse 25. "He shall speak as if he were God" So Jerome quotes from Symmachus. "To none can this apply so well and so fully as to the popes of Rome. They have assumed infallibility, which belongs only to God. They profess to forgive sins, which belongs only to God. They profess to open and shut heaven, which belongs only to God. They profess to be higher than all the kings of the earth, which belongs to God. Moreover, they go beyond God in pretending to loose whole nations from their oath of allegiance to their kings, when such kings do not please them.
>
> In addition, they go against God when they give indulgences for sin. "This is the worst of all blasphemies." (Adam Clarke, *Commentary* on *the Old Testament*). Vol. 1V, p. 596, note on (*Daniel* 7:25) (*Ibid.*, pp 114, 115).

Friends it is blasphemous and dangerous for anyone to usurp the honor and reverence that belong to God. As humans, we are all subject to err. We were all born in sin, and we all need God's mercy and forgiveness. There is nowhere in scripture where God gave human the power to forgive sins. The word of God says, sin is the transgression of the law, and this law, is the law of God. Think for a moment; is it possible for someone to forgive another for hurting you, on your behalf? How is it then possible for someone to forgive your sins on behalf of God?

This little horn power represented by the papacy, would rival the title, and honor due to God. Paul describes this power as the man of sin. "He exalts himself by opposing all those who truly worship God. He will set himself in the midst of the church and speak for God as if he were God" (*2 Thessalonians* 2:4).

The following extracts will signify the extent to which the Papacy has gone in their claim for titles not meant for humans. Most of which are from Catholic writers.

"All names in the Scriptures are applied to Christ, by virtue of which it is established that he is over the church, all the same names are applied to the Pope."-Robert Bellarmine, *Disputationes de Controversilis,* Tom. 2, "Controversia Prima." Book 2 ("De Conciliorum Auctoritate" [On the authority of Councils]), chap 17 (1628 ed. Vol. 1, p.266) translated (*Bible Reading* p.82).

"For thou art the shepherd, thou art the physician, thou art the husbandman; finally thou art another God on earth."—Christopher Marcellus Oration in the *Fifth Lateran Council 4th session.* In J.D. Mansi, Sacrorum Conciliorum . . . Collectio, vol. 32, col. 761, translated (*Ibid.*, p.83).

Little Horn to, "Wear Out the Saints of the Most high."

Historical investigation proves that Rome, during the time of antiquity, and the Dark Ages, carried out great work of destruction against the church of God. After the great work of Reformation, wars, massacres, crusades, inquisitions, and persecutions of various kinds, were used to compel all to submit to the Roman yoke. Albert Barns asks a very pertinent question:

"Can anyone doubt that this is true of the papacy?" He went on to list some of the atrocities Protestants endured before and after the Reformation. These include, The Inquisition, 'the persecutions of the Waldenses;' the ravages of the Duke of Alva; the fires of Smithfield; the tortures of

Goa—indeed, the whole history of the papacy may be appealed to in proof that this is applicable to that power." (*Daniel and the Revelation* p.115).

He went on further to say, "If anything could have 'worn out the saints of the Most High'—could have cut them off from the earth so that evangelical religion would have become extinct, it would have been the persecution of the papal power" (*Ibid*, p. 115 para 4).

> In the year 1208, a crusade was proclaimed by Pope Innocent III against the Waldenses, and Albigenses, in which a million men perished. From the inception of the order of the Jesuits in the year, 1540-1580, nine hundred and fifty thousand perished by the Inquisition. In the Low Countries, fifty thousand persons met cruel deaths, some were hanged, others beheaded, and some were burned, and some were buried alive, for the crime of heresy. All these atrocities occurred within the space of thirty-eight years from the edict of Charles the V against the Protestants, to the peace of Chateau Cambreses in 1559. Eighteen thousand were executed in the space of five and half years during the administration of the Duke of Alva . . . [21]

Anyone acquainted with the history of the papacy will agree that what is said about, "making war with the saints" (*verse* 21), and "wearing out the saints of the Most High" (*verse* 25), describe without a doubt its history, and without question applies to that power for what it truly is.

Albert Barnes, *Notes on Daniel*, p. 328, comment on *Daniel* 7: 25). W. E. H. Lecky, agrees:

> That the Church of Rome has shed more innocent blood than any other institution that has ever existed among mankind, will be questioned by no Protestant who has a complete knowledge of history. The memorials, indeed of many of her persecutions

are now so scanty that it is impossible to form a complete multitude of her victims, and it is quite certain that no powers of imaginations can adequately realize their suffering . . . These atrocities were not perpetrated in the brief paroxysms of a reign of terror, or by the hand of obscure sectaries, but were inflicted by a triumphant church, with every circumstance of solemnity and deliberation. [22]

"Many times the victims were turned over to the civil authorities, but because the church made the decision about heresy, it made no difference. Secular powers then were under the decision of the church and did its bidding."

Cardinal Bellarmine a Catholic inadvertently admitted to Luther that the Catholic Church burned or otherwise put to death an infinite number of heretics. Another Catholic said,

When confronted by heresy, she does not content herself with persuasion; argument of an intellectual and moral order appear insufficient, and she has recourse to force, to corporal punishment, to torture. She creates tribunals like those of the Inquisition, she calls the laws of the state to her aid, if necessary she encourages a crusade, or a religious war, and all her 'horror of blood' practically culminates into urging the secular power to shed it, which proceeding is almost more odious—for it is less frank—than shedding it herself . . . [23]

Rulers like, Francis 1 of France, Henry II of England under Mary Tudor, tortured heretics, and actively encouraged and aided the religious wars.

In **A.D. 1417-1431**, Pope Martin the V, sent the following letter to the king of Poland:

Know that the interest of the Holy See, and those of your crown, make it a duty to exterminate the Hussites. Remember that these impious persons dare proclaim principles of equality; they maintain that all Christians are brethren, and that God has not given to privileged men the right of ruling the nations; they hold that Christ came on earth to abolish slavery; they call the people to liberty, that is, to the annihilation of kings and priests! Whilst there is still time, then, turn your forces against Bohemia; burn, massacre, make deserts everywhere, for nothing could be more agreeable to God, or more useful to the cause of kings, than the extermination of the Hussites. [24]

(For more on the Hussites see Appendix D)

Pagan Rome persecuted the Christian Church mercilessly and it is estimated that three million individuals perished in the first three centuries of the Christian era. Ironically these Christians prayed for the continuance of imperial Rome, for they knew, that the power that would succeed them, would be worst than they were. They knew that a persecuting power would arise that would, "wear out the saints of the Most High," as was declared in prophecy. (See Appendix E)

Pagan Rome would spare the mother and kill the baby, but papal Rome slew both mother and baby. Nothing would appeal to their conscience so they would show mercy, no age, sex, condition of health, nothing that would make an exemption from the relentless rage of Rome.

From the above references, it is clear; Rome cruelly punished those who dare to utter a dissenting voice against her teachings. The deadly wound it was dealt in 1798, is being healed, for the Bible said it would. Therefore, there will be a repeat of history of a greater magnitude of such cruelty and blood shed as was not experienced before. The church is vying to establish unity of church and state. When this is done, there will not be any grit in government to withstand the unfair demands that will be placed upon people, especially those who dare to oppose the Roman Church.

All that is needed, is for the curtain to be pulled but just a little to see the subtle masks this religious group is wearing to pretend to want unity for the families of the world. Do not be alarmed my good reader, open your eyes, know the times.

No man can bring world peace. If they try, they are defying God for the stone Daniel saw that filled the whole world, which is Christ's kingdom is the only One that can bring world peace. Can it be that those who try may have esoteric agendas?

Charlemagne united medieval Europe through secret societies. The hierarchical power of the Roman Catholic Church gives its head, the pope, authority over Roman Catholics over the world. Consider how easy it would be to pass laws if the pope were to enact them or to agree to their enactment. This would be especially true of those popes who the people consider pious and humble.

Kings of the earth are cooperating with Rome to globalize the nations to bring about civil unity. Notwithstanding, unity of the nations will only happen when Jesus sets up His kingdom, not before and not by any well-meaning individual or organization. Iron and clay cannot cleave. Anyone who tries to do this will be fighting a losing battle and defying God's words.

The churches are in unity with Rome for religious freedom through the ecumenical movement. Nothing is wrong in wanting to unite people and nations, and to have peace, but for what reason? Is it so one body, person, or organization has centralized power? The Vatican recently called for a controlling body to manage global finances. Please take note that many of the earth's resources are central to the global plan.

Many are advocating for globalization, thinking it is a good way of managing and sharing scarce resources, (if controlled by honest hearts) but the very opposite is a frightening reality. Think for a moment what globalization means, it is a way of centralizing (in this case resources) for the best good of those concerned. What if the person or organization in charge favors some over others, what would happen to the less favored? Centralization will make the passing of laws (like the Sunday observance) easier, and this is not "if" but "when." Watch for the signs and be aware.

Little Horn to think to change Times and Laws

Religio-politico organizations have tried to change times, by attempting to begin the week with Monday instead of Sunday, but this brought about much confusion and controversy so they returned to the original, Sunday as the beginning of the week. Jesus confirmed that there are twelve hours in a day by the question He asked in *John* 11: 9 "Are there not twelve hours in a day?" Rome changed that to twenty-four hours, so instead of the day ending at sunset and the next beginning thereafter, the day ends at midnight, which would have made this new day already six or more hours late (depending on the sunset hour).

Governments sometimes change laws to suit changing circumstances. The little horn claims it has the power to change laws as far as its jurisdiction extends, but these laws are not human laws. These laws belong to the God of heaven to whom the saints belong. The papacy has attempted to change the laws of God by combining the first and second commandments and dividing the tenth into two. Hence, the ninth forbids the coveting of a neighbor's wife, while the tenth the neighbor's property.

The Roman Catholic Catechism, authorized by the Council of Trent, explains that the images and likeness thereof mentioned by the second commandment, the making and use are allowed except that of God Himself. These they say, venerate the virtues of the saints, and not to worship them as gods. "The same explanation is given for the bones, ashes and other relics of saints and to representations of angels."

THE TEN COMMANDEMENTS *Exodus 20:3-17*

1.	*Thou shall have no other gods before Me*
2.	*Thou shalt not make unto thee any graven image, or any likeness of anything that is in the heaven above, or that is in the earth beneath, or that is in the waters under the earth: thou shalt not bow down thyself to them, nor serve them: for I the Lord thy God am a jealous God, visiting the iniquity of the fathers upon the children unto the third and fourth generation of them that hate Me ; and showing mercy to thousands of them that love Me and keep My commandments.*
3.	*Thou shalt not take the name of the Lord thy God in vain; for the Lord will not hold him guiltless that taketh His name in vain.*
4.	*Remember the Sabbath day, to keep it holy, Six days shalt thou labor and do all thy work: but he seventh day is the Sabbath of the Lord thy God: in it thou shalt not do any work thou, nor thy son, nor thy daughter, thy manservant nor thy maidservant, nor thy cattle, nor thy strange that is within thy gates: for in six days the Lord made heaven and earth, the sea and all that in them is and rested on the seventh day, wherefore the Lord blessed the Sabbath day and hallowed it.*
5.	*Honor thy father and thy mother: that thy days may be long upon the land which the Lord thy God giveth thee.*
6.	*Thou shalt not kill.*
7.	*Thou shalt not commit adultery.*
8.	*Thou shalt not steal.*
9.	*Thou shalt not bear false witness against thy neighbor.*
10.	*Thou shalt not covet thy neighbor's house, thou shalt not covet thy neighbor's wife, nor his manservant, nor his maidservant, nor his ox, nor his ass, nor anything that is thy neighbor's.*

THE TEN COMMANDMENTS
As Abbreviated in Vernacular Roman Catchisms

1. *I am the Lord thy God. Thou shall not have strange gods before Me.*

2. *Thou shalt not take the name of the Lord thy God in vain.*

3. *Remember thou keep holy the Sabbath day.*

4. *Honor thy father and thy mother.*

5. *Thou shalt not kill.*

6. *Thou shalt not commit adultery.*

7. *Thou shalt not steal.*

8. *Thou shalt not bear false witness against thy neighbor.*

9. *Thou shalt not covet thy neighbor's wife.*

10. *Thou shalt not covet thy neighbor's goods.*

The fourth commandment is numbered as the third in their arrangement. The Catechism, the highest authority in the Roman Catholic Church, keeps the entire commandments and urges its observance in both private life and public worship as a sacred duty and privilege (*Treasures of Life* p. 121).

This however, does not refer to the seventh day of the week. They claim this was a part of the ceremonial laws of the Jews and was nailed to the cross. This sabbath refers to the first day of the week, and the church gives reasons why the Sabbath should be observed on the first day of the week called Sunday.

According to *The Catholic Encyclopedia*, "The authority of this catechism is higher than that of any other, but is, of course, not on the level of the canons and decree of a council" (*Daniel and the Revelation* p.121). The Roman Catholic Church holds that the canons and decrees of an ecumenical church council are both official and supreme. Among such councils is the Council of Trent, held in Italy, from 1545-1563. *"Catholic Encyclopedia, art,* Doctrine, Christian," Vol. V, p. 79.

The following is a quote taken from the fifth edition of the Roman Catechism, about the fourth commandment, the (Catholic third) published in Rome in 1796 . . .

It pleased the church of God, that the religious celebration of the Sabbath day should be transferred to 'to the Lord's day' [meaning Sunday]; for as on that day light first shone on the world; so by the resurrection of our Redeemer on that day, who opened to us the gate to eternal life, our life was recalled out of darkness into light, whence also the Apostles would have, it named 'the Lord's day'. We also observed in the Sacred Scripture that this day was held sacred because on that day the creation of the world commenced, and the Holy Ghost was given to the apostles.[25] Catechism of the Council of Trent, p. 4.

The above-mentioned statements sufficiently show the intention of the papacy to think to change times and laws. By their own declaration, the Roman Catholic changed the time for Sabbath observance from the seventh day of the week, which by scripture is called, "The Lord's Day," to the first day of the week. All the reasons they give for the change are of human origin and ecclesiastical invention.

The declaration by the church is enough to prove that the papacy has thought to change times and laws. They have openly and boldly declared that they have changed the day, and even go as far as to taunt Protestants for accepting and observing the change (*Mark of the Beast in Revelation* 13, (*Daniel and the Revelation* p.125, 560-564).

Those Protestants, who embrace the observance of the first day instead of the seventh, should really review, and change their name; for how can they be protesting against the policies of the church yet are worshipping on the same day as those who change the day of worship. Through the Roman Catholic Catechism, they state categorically that the Sabbath commandment teaches Sunday observance: (Note keenly the answers to questions on the Catholic change of the Sabbath to Sunday observance).

Q. Say the Third Commandment.
A. Remember that thou keep holy the Sabbath day.
Q. What is commanded by the Third Commandment?
A. To sanctify the Sunday (*Treasures of Life* p.560).

Have you seen that this is a direct contradiction of the Bible? *Exodus* 20;8-11 say among other things, God blessed the Sabbath and hallowed it. *Malachi* 3:6, says God does not change, in *Revelation* 22: 18,19, a warning is given to anyone who adds or takes away from the word of God, and in

Matthew 5:19, Jesus says anyone who breaks and teaches shall be called least in the kingdom. Dear reader God will have nothing but the best, He will have all or none at all. According to *James* 2:10, anyone who offends in one point is guilty of breaking the whole law.

A New Catechism of Christian Doctrine and Practice, records the following:

Q. What day was the Sabbath?

A. The seventh day, or Saturday.

Q. Do you keep the Sabbath?

A. No, we keep the Lord's Day

Q. Which is that?

A. The first day: Sunday.

Q. Who changed It?

A. The Catholic Church.

James Bellord, A New Christian Catechism of Christian Doctrine and Practice pp. 86, 87 in (Treasures of Life p. 561).

A popular *Baltimore Catechism records* the following question and answer:

Q. Are the Sabbath day and Sunday the same?

A. The Sabbath day and Sunday are not the same. The Sabbath day is the seventh day of the week, and is the day, which was kept holy in the old law; the Sunday is the first day of the week, and is the day, which is kept holy in the new law.

The Catholic Christian Instructed records this:

Q. What warrant you for keeping the Sunday preferably to the ancient Sabbath, which was Saturday?

A. We have for it the authority of the Catholic Church, and apostolic tradition.

Q. Does the Scripture anywhere command the Sunday to be kept for the Sabbath?

A. The Scripture commands us to hear the church (*Matt.*18:17: *Luke* 10; 16), and to hold fast the traditions of the apostles (*2 Thess.* 2: 15), but the Scriptures do not in particular mention this change of the Sabbath."

The reader must note that God does not change, neither has He given anyone power or authority to change anything from His words. Anyone or organization who does so, is really going against what God has said, and this could be seen as defiance. Please note also, that the Ten Commandment, (of which the fourth, is the Sabbath and is a part) was written by God Himself, the only entry the Bible declares that God has written Himself. *Exodus* 31:18 "And He gave unto Moses, when He had made an end of communing with him upon Mount Sinai, two tables of stone, **written with the finger of God."**

Deuteronomy 4: 13, "And He declared unto you His covenant, which He commanded you to perform, even ten commandments; and **He wrote them upon two tables of stone."** It would seem that this law is very important to God, the fact that He took the time to write it Himself, not once but twice.

Exodus 34: 1 "And the Lord said unto Moses, Hew thee two tables of stone like unto the first: and **I will write** upon these tables the words that were in the first tables, which thou breakest."

Malachi 3:6, "For I am the Lord I change not; therefore ye sons of Jacob are not consumed."

> For verily I say unto you, till heaven and earth pass one
> jot, or one title shall in no wise pass from the law, till all be

fulfilled. Whosoever therefore shall break one of these least commandments, and shall teach men so, he shall be called least in the kingdom of heaven: but whosoever shall do and teach them, the same shall be called great in the kingdom of heaven (*Matthew* 5: 18, 19).

It is a mistake to think that the commandment breaker will be in heaven, only he occupies a lower place. This could not be, for God says if we break one we are guilt of all. No guilty person will enter the gates of heaven. All guilt must be confessed now, and Jesus will clear the guilty of all wrongdoing. Now is the time for that to happen. Jesus invites us to come right now, not tomorrow, not the next day, now. No one knows what a day brings, and there is no repentance in the grave, or after the resurrection. The dead is unconscious, cannot repent, neither can anyone pray for the dead (*Ecclesiastics* 9:5,6). Remember there is no least in the kingdom of heaven. Jesus only accepts one hundred percent, so a least person will not be in heaven, for the same reason, he /she did not measure up to full percentage.

Jesus is waiting on you to come. *Revelation* 3: 20, says, "Behold I stand at the door and knock: if any man hear my voice, and open the door, I will come in to him and sup with him, and he with me." It is not courteous to have Jesus waiting. He has a reward for those who love Him. Conversely, there will be wages for those who will be least, for they had not loved or obeyed His instructions.

We have a choice to either love Jesus by our obedience to His commandments and be rewarded with eternal life, and be inside the city, or reject Him by disobeying His commandments and receive the wages for disobedience, and be eternally lost. It is true the commandments cannot save anyone, it is Jesus who saves, but the saved ones take pleasure in keeping His commandments. The commandments should not be kept to be saved, but the saved keep the commandments. He loves you and really wants to save you. (*John* 3: 16) He saves the sinner from sin, not in sin. He really loves you that is why He died. Will you love Him in return? (*John* 14:15).

Revelation 22: 14,15, say, "Blessed are they that do His commandments, that they may have right to the tree of life, and may enter in through the gates into the city." Those who keep the commandments of God are "blessed." John says some will be outside: "For without are dogs and sorcerers, and whoremongers, and murderers, and idolaters, and whosever loveth and maketh a lie."

Many people are not aware that in defending the Sunday observance, they are in fact, obeying the commandments of men, found in the Catechism of the Council of Trent. Speaking about the commandment, referring to Sunday as his day says the following, "Sunday is our mark of authority . . . The church is above the Bible and this transference of Sabbath observance is proof of that fact" (Catholic Record Sept. 1,1923).

The following statement was taken from a Jesuit Magazine: "The old Protestant culture is about at the end of the rope . . . Why can't we make the US Catholic Legislation, Catholic in justice, aims and ideals?" (Father F.X. Talbot, editor of America, official Jesuit Magazine for, US, NY Globe). It is neither strange nor alarming for doing well, being obedient, upholding high standards to be called, "old." Be warned "latest" is not always the best. When it comes to your salvation, test your decision by the word of God (*Isaiah* 8:20).

My dear reader, do you understand the marrow of this statement? It is no wonder this organization claims to have authority to change the day of worship from Sabbath to Sunday. The leaders give themselves authority based on tradition and manmade rules, in other words they are law unto themselves. How could anyone place tradition over God's word, when *Psalm* 138:2 says God magnifies His word above all His name?

After being exposed to such information what system will you give Center Stage in your life? Is it tradition or the Bible? The council to those who really love the Lord is to break away fully from manmade systems and traditions, and adhere to the Bible and the Bible only in belief and practice.

In *Revelation* 18: 4, God calls those who love Him to come out of Babylon or false teachings and false worship. Anyone who participates in her wrongs will partake of her punishment. Let me hasten to say, though the system is wrong, there is hope for the people. God is calling you to leave the system, because it is not of Him. The system of worship is in defiance of the command of God. He loves everyone and wants you to worship him who made heaven and earth.

[18&19]   Treasures of Life p.523, 524.

[20]   Ibid., p.114.

[21]   Ibid., p.115 para. 2).

[22]   Ibid, p.117 para. 2

[23]   & [24] Ibid., p.119.

[25]   Ibid p.124.

CHAPTER 18

Three and a Half Years

According to the Bible, a day in prophecy stands for one year *(Ezekiel* 4:6; *Numbers* 14:34). One of the ecclesiastical figures of the twelfth century, Joachim, abbot of Calabria, applied the year-day principle to the 1260-year period.

A Time and Times and the Dividing of Time.

In *Daniel* 4:23 "time" is one year; therefore, "times" would be two years. *Daniel* 7:25 last part says, until a time and times and the dividing of time. The dividing of time is "a half," according to the Septuagint translation. The beast would exercise its power for three and a half years. The reader must note we are now dealing with symbolic prophecy, which means the measurement of time is not literal (Remember *Daniel* is a prophetic book) (See Appendix F).

The woman clothed with the sun, who signifies the church, remained hidden in the wilderness from the face of the serpent, a day without doubt being accepted for a year and a thousand and two hundred and sixty days for the same number of years. Joachim of Floris, Concordantia, book 2, chapter 16, p. 12b.

Sir Isaac Newton concurred with this statement:

Three times and a half; that is, for 1260 solar years, reckoning a time for a calendar year of 360 days, and a day for a solar year. After which 'the judgment is to sit, and they shall take away his dominion,' not at once, but by degrees, to consume, and to destroy it unto the end. [26]

Revelation 11:3 "And I will give power unto my two witnesses, and they shall prophesy a thousand two hundred and three score days, clothed in sackcloth."

Take note, the Bible year is three sixty days, (**360x 3=1080** add **half of 360** to that = **1080 plus 180 = 1260**), which is equivalent to three and a half years (31/2 prophetic years). The question is, "Did the papacy possess dominion that length of time?" The answer is a resounding "yes." History records that the papal power persecuted the church for 1260 years, dating from the period **538 A.D.-1798 A. D.** Simple calculations make this exactly 1260 years.

A proclamation from emperor Justinian, in **A. D. 533** gave power and authority to the bishop of Rome the head of all the churches. This edict was not executed until Rome had finally extirpated the last of the three kingdoms. The little horn replaced the up rooted kingdoms. This makes perfect sense for in earlier chapters on "The Little Horn" power, it was noted, that of the kingdoms represented by the image in *Daniel* 2: 32-33, the head of gold represented Babylon. The breast and arms of silver represented Medo-Persia, belly and thighs of brass represented Greece, legs of iron represented Rome, the feet were partly iron and partly clay, represented ten divided kingdoms.

It was three of the ten kingdoms that would be uprooted and give place to the little horn. In **A.D. 493**, the Heruli were eradicated, and so were the Vandals between **A.D. 533** and **534**, when Justinian entered upon the Vandals and Gothic wars. Suffice it to say, though the Roman bishop was granted permission by Justinian to take charge, he could not, if any of the three horns remained in place. Therefore, the Arian Ostrogoths the last of the three kingdoms (that were to be plucked to make room for the papacy), was driven from Rome, and this was accomplished in the year **A.D. 538.**

For 1**260** years, Rome ruled the world with an iron fist, but the close of this prophecy, came exactly at the end of **1798**. Berthier along with a French army entered Rome and took the pope prisoner. Hence, a deadly wound was inflected to the papacy, just as the prophecy had predicted. Since that time the church enjoyed partial religious freedom. This is not to encourage complacency in any way, because much of this freedom is gradually diminishing, because very stealthily Rome is being restored to its former strength. The deadly wound is beginning to heal.

> Revelation 13:3 says "And I saw one of the heads of this sea beast suddenly go limp as if it had been fatally wounded. This greatly affected the beast and it looked as if it would bleed to death. However, suddenly the wound was healed and it was well again. Then I saw the beast begin to walk the earth. Everywhere it went; people were influenced by its charm" (See Chapter 16).

Deadly Wound Healed.

As the deadly wound started to heal, papal life slowly but surely gained momentum towards the beginning of the **1800**, when a new pope was elected. The palace and temporal dominion over the Papal States were restored. The only thing he could not do was to be a systematic prosecutor. Men will usurp authority as much as they are allowed by God to do, but they can only do so much, and no more. They have no power by themselves, all their actions are limited. One thing is certain, the word of God must be fulfilled (*Daniel and the Revelation* p.131).

Daniel 7:26 says "The judgment shall sit, and they shall take away his dominion, to consume and destroy it to the end." Judgment began in the heavenly sanctuary in **1844**, according to the latter part of verse 10, of Daniel 7 . . . "The judgment was set and the books were opened." In verse 11, there is evidence that the beast was slain because of the words of the horn.

In **1854** the doctrinal system of the Immaculate Conception was decreed by the pope, and in **1870**, the temporal power of the pope was taken away, by the armies of Victor Emmanuel. This was the very year the Ecumenical Council decreed the infallibility of the pope (See Chapter 17). Despite this and other honors heaped on the office of the bishop of Rome by the clergy, his temporal power was taken away. The popes shut themselves in the Vatican of Rome as prisoners, until the signing of the concordat with Italy. However, in **1929** the Lateran Treaty restored temporal power to the pope including "his dominion" over sections of Rome, and especially the Vatican City.[27]

Daniel 7:27, "Then God's people will be given their own kingdom, taking in the whole world, every country under heaven." God's people are optimistic in His promises for the future, but to inherit we must continue to be faithful. "It will be exclusively for God's people and will last forever. It will be governed by the Most High God, and everyone there will obey and serve Him from a loving heart." Verse 28 "This ended our conversation. I was greatly perplexed at what I had seen, and my face turned pale. But I kept it all to myself."

After beholding the grim and desolate picture of what the papacy would do to the saints of the Most High God, the prophet's eyes were directed to a glorious period of rest for God's children. They shall inherit the kingdom free from all oppressive powers. These glorious promises are great to look forward to, despite the trials and injustice meted out to God's people, a better day is coming. Glory be to God! Hallelujah! This is something to look forward to, never mind the foaming billows of trials and temptations, with Christ in the vessel we can smile at the storm. Remember Jesus will make a way.

[26] Sir Isaac Newton, *Observations upon the Prophecies of Daniel*, pp. 127, 128.
[27] Ibid, p. 131.

CHAPTER 19

Daniel's Second Dream

In the third year of Belshazzar's reign Daniel had a dream. The events of the dream took place on the banks of the river Ulai. In the dream, he saw a ram with two horns, one horn was higher than the other and he was pushing westward, northward, and southward; and no beast could stand before him. While still looking at the ram, a he goat with an extraordinary horn between his eyes came from the west and did not touch the ground (*Daniel* 8:1-5).

The reader must remember that, the first kingdom of Nebuchadnezzar's dream was Babylon, overthrown and taken by Medo-Persia, the ram with two horns. The he goat, which attacked it, was Greece, and the power that succeeded Greece was Rome. Compare these facts with Nebuchadnezzar's image of Daniel 2, and the vision of chapter 7. In these accounts it is clear that every succeeding power is more powerful in their attack than the one before. Hence, Rome's attack would be more powerful than Greece, even though Greece was more powerful than Medo-Persia.

This goat ran towards the ram and attacked him with great force and broke his horns, hit him to the ground and stamped on him. His horn finally broke and four horns came up in its place, which pointed in four directions. A little horn came out of one of them and showed great power towards the south. This was true of Rome. Egypt became a province of Rome in **30 B.C.** and was for many centuries. Note that Egypt is in the south.

- The little horn became great towards the east. Rome conquered Syria in **65 B.C.**, and made it a province.
- The little horn became great towards "the pleasant land." Rome did that. The pleasant land refers to Judea (*Deuteronomy* 8:7, 11: 10, 11: *Ezek.* 20: 6, *Ps.* 106: 24). The Romans also made it a province in **63 B.C.** and after some time destroyed the city and the temple and scattered the Jews over the world. [28]

This horn even threw down some of the stars of heaven, and trampled on them. (*Verses* 9, 10) In figure Rome did that too. The following verse said he magnified himself to the prince of the "host" and their leaders, symbolically, "host" refers to the people of God, and the place of their worship. In Revelation we read that the great red dragon a symbol of Satan, cast down the third part of the stars to the ground (*Revelation* 12: 3-6). The little horn even magnified himself to the Prince of the host. Verse 11," Yea, he magnified himself even to the prince of the host, and by him the daily sacrifice was taken away, and the place of his sanctuary was cast down."

[12] "And a host was given him against the daily sacrifice by reason of transgression, and it cast down the truth to the ground; and it practiced and prospered."

From the time of the reign of Seleucus, king of Persia, until the country was conquered by the Romans, twenty-six kings, subjugated the country ruled at different periods over the territory. These kings represented the "horn" of the goat. The little horn was very great, and was to stand up against the Prince of princes, a title that without the shadow of a doubt refers to Jesus Christ.

What is the Daily?

This question implies that the events to which the vision relates occupies a series of years. The "daily" represents the complete time of the vision, and "transgression of desolation." This therefore means the daily cannot refer to the ceremonial sacrifice of the Jews, (for at the fullness of time or at the crucifixion of Jesus, the animal sacrifice would cease. The cessation of animal sacrifice occurred when Jesus was crucified and the veil of the temple was rent in two from top to bottom) if that were so the daily would be limited to a short period up to that point, but the daily must be continuing over a period of years.

There are three interpretations for the daily, and the one most often used by Bible scholars means—"continual," and this means the priestly ministry of Jesus in the heavenly sanctuary is continuing. *(Hebrews 7:25 and 1 John 2:1)* Jesus is making intercession for those who come to Him, and He is our advocate when we sin. [29]

The daily also represents papal substitution. The substitution of the papacy include:

- *The substitution of allegiance to the pope*, instead of to Christ.
- *Compulsory unity of the visible church*, instead of the voluntary unity of all believers in the body of Christ.
- *The authority of the visible head of the church, the pope*, instead of, that of Christ the invisible head of the church.
- *A priestly hierarchy*, instead of direct access to Christ by believers.
- *A system of salvation by works*, instead of salvation by faith in Christ.

- *In addition, the confessional and sacrifice of the mass*, in place of the meditatoral work of Christ as our great High Priest in heaven.
- *The Doctrine of the natural immortality of the soul* instead of the resurrection and general judgments.

These substitutions have diverted men's attention from Christ, thus depriving them of the benefits of His ministry.[30]

Two Desolating Powers

The little horn symbolizes Rome in its two phases, **pagan** and **papal** Rome. In the third interpretation of the daily, these phases are the daily in some places, and the transgression of desolation in other places. The **daily** refers to pagan Rome and the **transgression of desolation** to the **papal** Rome. [31] (See Appendix G).

It was pagan Rome in **A.D. 70** that destroyed the Temple in Jerusalem thereby ending its services. Rome in its pagan phase warred against the Jewish people and the early Christians. In its papal phase even to our day, Rome will be warring against the true church (*Daniel* 8: 13, 23).

Rome meets all areas of the prophecy like no other; hence, Rome is the power of the little horn. The inspired description given in the word of God of the nature and character of this religious system are exact, and the prophecies accurately fulfilled in history.

In verse *12 of Daniel 8,* we notice, a "host was given him against the daily." "Host," here is the same as, "army," being interpreted as the "multitudes" or "army."

> *Revelation* 13: 2 says of the dragon, And the beast, which I saw, was like unto a leopard, and his feet were as the feet of a bear, and his mouth as the mouth of a lion: and the dragon gave him

his power, and his seat, and great authority," that fell under the influence of this power.

The little horn would become mighty, but not of its own power (*Daniel* 8:24).

Rome lost its position as the place of worship, because in **A.D. 330**, Constantine removed the seat of government to Constantinople, thus fulfilling the prophecy of *Revelation* 13. The dragon pagan Rome gave his seat to the beast, papal Rome. It is well to note that, the **dragon** refers to **pagan Rome**, while the **beast** is the name given to **papal Rome**. His seat is the city of Rome.

The barbarians that weakened the Roman Empire, in the changes and transformation of those times, were converted to the Catholic faith, which contributed to the dethronement of their former religion. Though they conquered Rome politically, they were subjugated by Rome's theology, who themselves became perpetuators of the same empire in another phase. In other words, they enabled a system that would work to their ruin.

Rome always finds ways of carrying out her plans, using means that are working sometimes not easily detected as selfish and dangerous. Little did these people know that the same power they were upholding would one day harm them. One writer said, "This was brought about by reason of the "transgressions;" that is by the working of the mystery of iniquity. The papacy maybe called a system of iniquity because it has done its evil work, under the pretense of pure and undefiled religion." [32]

In the same verse 12, of *Daniel* 8, the little horn, "cast down the truth to the ground: and it practiced and prospered." Of this false religious system, Paul in 2 *Thessalonians* 2:7 wrote, "This mystery of lawlessness is already at work and will continue to spread until the one behind it is exposed and taken out of the way." "The little horn "cast down the truth to the ground, and practiced and prospered."

Practiced and Prospered:

He exalted himself and even took away the daily sacrifice and threw down the place of the sanctuary. All the wrongs this little horn is doing to God's truth and is prospering, will soon end, and he will be exposed. Rome practiced its deceptions on the people. This power has practiced its schemes of cunning in order to reach its own goals and advance its power. It also has prospered. It has successfully made war against the saints and prevailed. It has almost done all it was predicted in prophecy to do. Soon it will be broken without hands, and the flames, would devour it to extinction in the consuming glories of the second appearing of our Lord.

Leo XlII made it clear to Catholics that it is their duty to bring back all civil society to the pattern and form of Christianity, which they have described.—*The Great Encyclical Letters of Leo* XIII, "Encyclical Letter *Immortale* Dei, Nov. 1, 1885" p.132.

Pope Pius XIII, on September 7, 1947, said, "The time for reflection and planning is past, in religious and moral fields, and the time for action has arrived." He further stated there are five points on which success in religion and morality depend:

- Religious culture
- The sanctifying of Sunday
- The saving of the Christian family
- Social justice and loyalty
- Truthfulness in dealing

Evening Star (Washington, D.C.). Sept. 8, 1947. [33]

The reader needs to realize that it is not by coincidence that the sanctifying of Sunday and the saving of Christian family are included in the ideas the Pope deem will bring religious success. This is part of their plan to mandate Sunday observance as the day of worship, and to use the saving of the family as one of the reasons.

> All the faithful of Christ must believe that the holy Apostolic See and Roman Pontif possesses *(sic)* The primacy over the whole world . . . and that full power was given to him in blessed Peter to rule, feed and govern the universal church by Jesus Christ our Lord

(. . . *Vatican Council*) (1870), ch. 3 . . . in Bible Readings p.83. How can they feed, rule and govern the world? Is it possible? Does globalization sound familiar? The other question is who will be in charged? (See Chapter 17). Remember no one has the right to use force in the choice of worship, Jesus does not force, and if any system uses force it is not of God.

Time in the Prophecy

The two previous verses of *Daniel* 8 ended the vision. The length of time the desolating powers previously mentioned, would be in effect, is most interesting and important. How long shall they continue to oppress and persecute God's people? This question would prove to be of paramount interest to the prophet and to the church. Two celestial beings conversed between themselves upon the subject. One asked the other, "How long shall be the vision concerning the daily sacrifice, and the transgression of desolation, to give both the sanctuary and the host to be trodden under foot?" Another saint replied,

> **"Unto two thousand three hundred sixty days: then shall the sanctuary be cleansed"** (*Verses* 13, 14).

The word sanctuary is not here referring to the temple in Jerusalem, for ancient history recorded that this temple would be destroyed. Pagan Rome had destroyed the temple in Jerusalem in **A. D.70**. The prophetic time of verse 14, was to extend to almost eighteen centuries beyond **A. D. 70**. This fact also shows that there was relationship between pagan and papal Rome (*Daniel* 7). Therefore "sanctuary," would have to be the sanctuary in heaven, "the tabernacle, which the Lord pitched, and not man," of which the sanctuary on earth was only a "shadow" (*Hebrews* 8: 2, 5).

The Jewish Day of Atonement was to them a day of judgment, which was in fact a type of the investigative judgment in heaven. The 2300 days in prophecy is 2300 years. A day in prophecy means a year (*Ezekiel* 4:6) This prophetic time would extend to the cleansing of the temple in heaven, or the investigative judgment. (See next chapter).

[28] *Treasures of Life p. 144.*

[29] *SDA Bible Commentary Vol.4 p. 843.*

[30] *Treasures of Life pp. 148, 149.*

[31] *Ibid, p. 145.*

[32] *Bible Reading p. 118.*

CHAPTER 20

Sanctuary to be Cleansed

Daniel 8: 14 speaks of the "sanctuary", which would not be referring to the temple in Jerusalem, because it was already destroyed, but instead refers to the sanctuary in heaven. *Hebrews* 8:2, 5 refer to it as, "the true tabernacle which the Lord pitched and not man," of which the sanctuary on earth was only a "shadow."

This subject requires close attention in order to understand the meaning and importance as to the beginning and ending of this great time prophecy. According to the prophet, it would be to the end of time. In addition, everyone should seek to understand when and where the "cleansing of the sanctuary" is to take place. All inhabitants of the earth have an interest in this solemn work, because whether we accept or reject it, we are all involved and it will have an impact on the inhabitants of the earth.

Many views are held concerning the location of the sanctuary, example the Earth, land of Canaan, the Church, and the Sanctuary in heaven. "The true tabernacle which the Lord pitched and not man," is "in heaven," and the Jewish tabernacle was a type, pattern or figure of that sanctuary. There are many conflicting views on the position of the sanctuary, therefore let the Bible be the only interpreter.

It Cannot Be the Earth

The word "sanctuary" is used in the Bible a total of one hundred and forty-four times. From its use in the Bible and the definitions given by lexicographers, we learn it is used to represent a holy or sacred place, a dwelling place for the Most High God. "If the earth is the sanctuary, then it should answer to all its definitions." The earth is neither holy, sacred, nor is it a place for the Most High.[33]

Colossians 3:2 says "Set your affection on things above, not on things on the earth." If the earth were the sanctuary where God's throne is, why would we be counseled not to set our love and interest on things on the earth? it clearly is not God's throne.

In *Isaiah* 66: 1 The Sovereign Lord says, "Heaven is My throne and earth is My footstool. What kind of house do you think you could build for me to rest in?" What kind of house can you build for Me that I can't build Myself?"(*CW*). The indication here is that God is sitting above in heaven and the earth is beneath Him, that is why the earth is His footstool.

2 *Peter* 3:10 says, "But the day of the Lord will come as a thief in the night: in the the heavens shall pass away with a great noise, and the elements shall melt with fervent heat, the earth also and the works that are therein shall be burned up."

The question is to anyone who thinks the earth is the sanctuary, "Why would God destroy a holy place, His dwelling place?" He would not, because the earth is not the sanctuary.

"Whereby are given unto us exceeding great and precious promises: that by these ye might be partakers of the divine nature, having escaped the corruption that is in the world through lust." Peter describes the world as corrupt, and God is going to one day destroy it (*2 Peter* 1: 4). Here is another clear reference that the earth could not be the sanctuary referred to, in the prophecy of *Daniel* 8:14.

Although God's sanctuary spoken of, in the above reference is not on earth, God's presence is here with His children. He surely does not leave nor forsake His children. *Exodus* 25:8, says, "And let them make Me a sanctuary; that I may dwell among them." It is clear God dwells with His people. Nevertheless, the temple revealed to John in *Revelation* 21:3, is not the same as the one Moses built. In the above-mentioned verse, that temple was temporary, but the temple of Revelation, exists after the heaven and earth are renewed. (*verse* 1) and will be permanent. "Behold the tabernacle of God is with men, and He will dwell with them, and they shall be His people, and God Himself shall be with them, and be their God." At present, this tabernacle of God is not on earth, but will be, after the purification of the earth, then the tabernacle of God will be with man and He will dwell with them.

Cannot Be the Land of Canaan

The following references are the closest in hinting that Canaan could be the sanctuary. However, exercise caution to interpret these references, for the Bible does not contradict itself. After many years of Egyptian bondage, the people of God were finally close to the land of promise. The passage through the Red Sea brought them closer home and Moses sang with a joyful heart . . . "You will bring your people into Canaan and plant them in that new land. You will bring them to the mountain of Your inheritance, to the country You have chosen for Yourself the place where Your temple will be built" (*Exodus* 15:17 CW).

Moses was anticipating what God would do for His people in the future. The Psalmist David picks up the prophecy and records it as history.

(*Psalm* 78:53, 54) "And He led them on safely, so that they feared not: but the sea overwhelmed their enemies. And He brought them to the border of His sanctuary, even to this mountain, which His right hand hath purchased." The "mountain" referred to here is the same as that in *Exodus* 15:17, by Moses. He said it was the border of the sanctuary, not the sanctuary.

The Psalmist makes it clear that Moses' reference to the sanctuary did not mean Canaan. He clearly said the mountain was the "border" of the sanctuary, and the sanctuary was built in that border or land. In 2 *Samuels* 5: 7 David took the strong hold of Zion and renamed it after him. This hill lay between Kidron and Tyropoeon. When David took the ark into the capital, Zion became the name of the place where God dwelt.

The sanctuary was built like high palaces, which would be referring to the beautiful, temple of the Jews, which was their center of worship. When Solomon built his temple, known as Zion, he placed the ark there. The names Israel and Jerusalem are interchangeable (*Isaiah* 40: 9; Ps. 48:1, 2). In conclusion, if Canaan were the sanctuary, it should not only be described as such, but the same idea should be established to the end, and purification of Palestine or the earth, should be known as the cleansing of the sanctuary. Indeed the earth is defiled and is to be purified, but this is not called the cleansing of the sanctuary, and this purification will not be done until after the second coming of Christ.[34]

It Cannot Be the Church

Psalm 114 1, 2, is the only reference that supports the notion that the church is the sanctuary. "When Israel went out of Egypt, the house of Jacob from a people of strange language; Judah was His sanctuary, and Israel His dominion." The literal interpretation of this text would suggest that the sanctuary was confined to one tribe only. This would also mean that only part of the church, and not the whole would be the sanctuary. God chose Jerusalem, which is in Judah to be the place of His sanctuary.[35]

Psalm 78:68 69 say "But chose the tribe of Judah, the mount Zion that *He* loved. And *He* built His sanctuary like palaces, like the earth which *He* established for ever" (*Emphasis supplied*).

God promised that He would build His sanctuary in the middle of the territory of that tribe, but the tribe itself was not the sanctuary. In *Daniel* 8: 13, 14, the sanctuary is something outstanding: "To give both the sanctuary and the host to be trodden underfoot." "Host" here mean the people of God. It is therefore clear that the sanctuary could not be the church. Indeed the temple was destroyed and trodden upon, but the people of God were protected even in perilous times.

[33] *Daniel and the Revelation* p. 151.

[34] Ibid, p. 152.

[35] Ibid, p. 155.

CHAPTER 21

The Sanctuary is the Temple in Heaven

> The whole point of what I have said is this: our new High Priest is so great that He took His seat at the right hand of the Majesty of heaven and earth. He is serving in the true Sanctuary, which is in heaven set by God and not by man *Hebrews* 8:1, 29 (*CW*).

Moses received a pattern of this Temple and Scripture bears explicit evidence on this point (*Hebrews* 9:1-5).

¹ Under the Levitical covenant, there were specific rules for worship connected with a fabricated Sanctuary. ² When the Levites put up the Sanctuary tent they placed the seven-branched candle stick and the table with consecrated bread behind the first curtain in the part called the Holy Place. ³ Behind the second curtain was that part of the Sanctuary called the Most Holy Place. ⁴ While the golden alter of incense was in the Holy Place, its function had to do with the Most Holy Place. In the Most Holy Place, itself was the golden Ark, inside of which was

the golden pot filled with manna, Aaron's rod that had budded and two tables of stones on which the Ten Commandments were written. [5]Above the Ark, were two beautifully carved angels one on each side, whose outstretched wings overshadowed the lids of the Ark called the Mercy Seat where the presence of God appeared. I can't take time just now to explain the meaning of each piece of furniture and the function of all and the Sanctuary service with which you are so familiar.

This account is definitely describing the tabernacle on earth erected by Moses. According to instructions from the Lord, the tabernacle had a holy place and a most holy place, and various articles used in the temple service. A full account of this temple is found in *Exodus* 25 and onward. If the reader is not acquainted with this building, the reader is encouraged to read the account. It is clear that from the references of *Hebrews* and *Exodus*, the temple in this context was the temple of the first covenant, which continued down to the time of the crucifixion of Christ.

The law required the life of the transgressor for his sins. Without the shedding of blood, there would be no absolution of sins. The blood of the slain victim was also a vehicle of its guilt. The priest used the blood to minister before God. The sprinkling of the blood by priest transferred the sins of the individual to the sanctuary. By these actions, the sanctuary became the receptacle of the sins of the people. At the end of every year, the accumulated guilt would be removed by a special service called the cleansing of the sanctuary, otherwise called the Day of Atonement. On this day, the priest would bring two goats, on which lots were cast to determine which one would be for the Lord. The other would be the scapegoat.

The goat chosen for the Lord would be killed and the blood sprinkled by the priest on the mercy seat. This was the only day of the year the priest had permission to enter the most holy place. As he came out of the temple he would, "lay both hands on the live goat and confess all the iniquities of the children of Israel." A fit man then took the scapegoat into the wilderness . . . and he shall let go the goat in the wilderness[36] (See also *Leviticus* 16: 8, 21, 22).

It was on one such days, as recorded in *Matthew* 27:50, 51 when on the cross, just before He died Jesus cried with a loud voice, that the veil of the temple between the holy and the most holy place was rent, thus exposing the inner apartment. (about the same time the priest was about to officiate these rites) Why was this?

Jesus' crucifixion

Jesus went to the cross, and He carried my sins with Him there. Thank God for Jesus. Thank You Jesus for Your love and sacrifice. He died willingly that a soul so unworthy might live.

Jesus the Lamb of God had now given His life to ransom the human race, and there was no more need for animal sacrifice, **type** had met **antitype.** The typical system was now done away by the great antitypical. The ceremony of the slaying of the goat, placing his blood on the mercy seat, the prayer and confession of the priest on behalf of the people, were all shadows of the ministry of Jesus in the heavenly sanctuary. Now that Jesus had accomplished His mission, of giving His life as a sacrifice for our sins, there was no more need, for these earthly ceremonies.[37]

Note the act of killing animals is **ceremony,** the death of Jesus on the cross, made these acts or ceremonies null and void. In fact, these were just types, which pointed to Jesus sacrificing His life on the cross for our sins. This act of sacrificing animals for sins was what the death of Jesus blotted out, the handwriting of ceremonies. In the same way we dishonor God if we were to sacrifice animals now for our sins, we dishonor Him if we misinterpret and teach our own understanding. Let the word of God interpret itself. "Blotting out the hand writing of ordinances that was contrary to us, and took it out of the way, nailing it to the cross" (*Colossians* 2: 14). His death blotted the ceremonies hand written by Moses, not His moral law that is a transcript of His character, and written by God, hence is unchangeable.

It is helpful to consider the services in the earthly sanctuary, for he served, "unto the example and shadow of heavenly things" (*Hebrews* 8:5). Both the temple in the wilderness and that of the heavenly had two main divisions, the **daily** and the **yearly**. The daily activities of Jesus as our High Priest were symbolized by the priest daily services. The annual Day of Atonement symbolized a work Christ would do in the heavenly sanctuary. An inspired writer writes of this event:

"The service of the earthly high priest was a shadow or a shadowy example of the real, which is the ministration of the Priestly work of Jesus." [38] Dear friends the daily sacrifice of the priest was a shadow of Jesus. Therefore, to conclude that there was no more need for animal sacrifice after the death of Jesus would be very accurate.

Paul now introduces Christ as "the mediator of a better covenant." If there is a better covenant, it implies there was one that was not the ideal, and that is a fair assumption, for the covenant, of animal sacrifice was not the ideal. The blood of these animals could not save anyone, they pointed forward to the spotless Lamb of God, who only could take away the sins of the sinner. So wouldn't you say that is a better plan, or covenant? In addition, He is also our mediator, and stands between God and us pleading for our sins.

"For there is one God, one mediator between God and men, the man Christ Jesus" (*1 Timothy* 2: 5). "As God, He understands God, and can speak for Him. As man He understands man and can sympathetically minister for him before the Father." Jesus is the only one who can forgive sins, therefore confession of sins should be to Him. No man can be or will ever be appointed for this very important work.

As in the typical service there was a work of atonement at the close of the year, so before Christ's work for the redemption of men is completed, there is a work of atonement for the removal of sin from the sanctuary. "The progress of this work should be the special concern of mankind." No one can ever deny that things cannot continue the way they are for much longer. "If people understood the bearing of these subjects on their eternal interests, they would give them their most careful and prayerful study."[39]

This is the service, which began in 1844, when the 2300 days ended. At that time, as foretold by Daniel the prophet, our High Priest began the solemn work of cleansing the sanctuary.

Anciently the sins of the people were by faith placed upon the sin offering and through its blood transformed in figure, to the earthly sanctuary, so in the new covenant the sins of the repentant, are by faith placed upon Christ and transferred, in fact to the heavenly sanctuary. In addition, as the typical cleansing of the earthly sanctuary was accomplished by the removal of the sins by which it had been polluted, so the actual cleansing of the heavenly sanctuary is to be accomplished by the removal, or blotting out, of the sins, which are there, recorded. [40]

However, before this can be accomplished, there must be an examination of the books of record to determine whom, through repentance and faith in Christ, are to benefit of His atonement. The cleansing of the sanctuary therefore involves a work of investigation—a work of judgment. This work must be performed prior to the coming of Christ to redeem His people. When He comes His reward is with Him to give to every man according to his works.[41]

Daniel 8:14 discloses the time for the commencement of this all-important work (that of cleansing of the sanctuary). It in co-operates the judgment which starts with the investigative phase and concludes with the executive phase. One very important component of the final judgment is the vindication of God's character before the inhabitants of the universe. All the false charges that Satan has laid against God as being unfair and harsh, must be proven false and groundless.

All those who had fallen prey to Satan, by believing his lies, and are to share his fate; they will realize they were deceived. They will acknowledge God, as just and fair, when it is late. In the mean time, those who trusted Jesus in hard times will be rejoicing in His salvation. Friends I feel strongly about the subject of our salvation, and the choices we make. If the choices we make are because they make us feel good, something is wrong with that. Jesus said He came to do the will of His Father. If we love the Lord, we should also do His will. If you really love Him, you will obey Him (See *John* 14:15).

The righteous will be singing, and the lost will be wailing, and moaning. Which of these groups would you rather? I sincerely hope you and I will be singing the song of Moses and the Lamb.

Revelation 15:3, 4 say

> They were singing the song of Moses and the Lamb a song of deliverance, saying, Great and wonderful are Your works, Lord God Almighty. Righteous and true are your ways King of nations. Who does not stand in awe of You? Who will not glorify Your name? You are the Holy One! All nations will kneel before you because they have seen what You have done and know that You have been gracious and just (Emphasis supplied).

Let us go back to the time of the crucifixion of Christ (*Matthew* 27: 50, 51).

"Jesus when He had cried again with a loud voice yielded up the ghost. [51] And, behold, the veil of the temple was rent in twain from the top to the bottom; and the earth did quake, and the rocks rent;" The veil of the temple was rent from top to bottom. This is an unusual occurrence, seeing things are ripped from bottom to top. In addition, this happened exactly at the time Jesus died.

The question is, why all this drama? It must be something to note. In *John* 19:30, Jesus said, "It is finished." To be finished means something started at some point.

Here is what one renowned writer says about this incident. When Christ cried out, "It is finished," all heaven triumphed. The controversy between Christ and Satan with regard to the execution of the plan of salvation was ended." [39] Christ claimed He had completed the conditions, now it was His Father's turn to fulfill the contract made in heaven concerning fallen man. Hence His words, "It is finished."

Jesus says in *John* 17: 4 "I have glorified Thee on the earth: I have finished the work which Thou gavest me to do."

This is very good news for the believer in Christ. Jesus had paid the ultimate price. He is now our Mediator between God and man.

"This is why Christ is the Mediator of the new covenant under which He paid the price for sin and set us free from the sentence of death. This payment was made not only for our sins, but also for the sins of those who lived under the Levitical covenant that they too may receive the promise of eternal inheritance by faith" (*Hebrews 9: 15*).

Christ's death on the cross benefited not only the people back then who once had to kill an animal, in order to pursue the process of repentance and forgiveness of sins. This also allows the post-cross inhabitants to access confession and forgiveness by going to God through Him, because He is the Mediator for the human race. Now, we do not depend on anyone to go to God on our behalf, we can go to Him through Jesus. Before the cross, this was not possible.

> *Verse 24 says*, That is why Christ who is the better Sacrifice, did not stay here to minister in the man-made Sanctuary on earth, which is only a copy of the true one in heaven, but entered heaven itself to appear in the presence of God, in our behalf, who is not confined to the Most Holy Place . . . (*CW*).

There is no more need for an earthly priest to represent us to God. The sinner needs to go to God through Christ for himself. He is our great high priest. *Hebrews* 8:1 says "The whole point of what I've said is this: our new High Priest is so great, that He took His seat at the right hand of the Majesty of heaven and earth."

Matthew 2:3, 4, 7, 12 reveal that Herod was troubled when he heard that one King of the Jews was born. He was determined to kill Him, so he asked the wise men to bring him news as to the location of this Baby.

However, being warned of God in a dream, not to go back to Herod, the wise men went home another way. Herod was not pleased that they had disobeyed him, so he set out to destroy all children two years and under. He knew that based on the time the wise men said they saw the star, the Baby could not be two years old, but he was ensuring that this Baby was dead, by widening his parameter.

> [16] When Herod heard that the teachers from the East had deliberately ignored him, he became violent. In his rage, he sent all the palace guards to kill all the babies in and around Bethlehem, who were two years old and under, basting his calculations for the child's age on the time the teachers from the East said they had first seen the star.

Here it is apparent that the enemy was trying to get Jesus at birth, and he continued to scheme and plot all the way to the cross. Satan and his work corrupted the affections of the children of men. If he had a chance to have uninterrupted power over mankind, it would have been death to the world. The implacable hatred he felt towards the Son of God surfaced in the way he treated Him while He was in the world. Christ's betrayal, trial, and crucifixion, were all planned by the fallen foe. His hatred carried out in the death of the Son of God, placed Satan where his true diabolical character revealed to all created intelligences the nature of the originator of sin (*Great Controversy* ch. 29).

Satan has tried for centuries to eradicate evidences for the authenticity of the sanctuary in heaven. Some believe it is not natural, and to hold that view, is to deny the work Christ is doing on our behalf for our salvation. Those who value and treasure the work of Jesus in the sanctuary on our behalf, need not fear, for no one can destroy this doctrine. "It is vouchsafed in Scripture forever." "The sanctuary . . . as the seat of God's government and His celestial dwelling place will continue through eternity." It is dangerous and damaging for anyone to materialize the things of heaven. There is conclusive evidence that there is a real heavenly sanctuary, where the throne of God is situated, surrounded by multitudes of angels, and our Great High Priest, Jesus Christ Himself (*Ibid.*, S.D.A. Bible Commentary v. 5, p. 1149).

[36] Great Controversy p. 371 and Daniel & Revelation p. 167).

[37] S.D.A Bible Commentary Vol. 5, p.1109.

[38] Daniel and the Revelation p. 167, 168.

[39] Ibid, p.170.

[40] Great Controversy pp.372, 373.

[41] Great Controversy p. 373.

Additional References

Heb. 10: 3-6, 9, 10, 12.

Heb. 9: 11-14.

Eph. 2:15.

CHAPTER 22

Ministration in Figuration and in Fact

The earthly priest served in both apartments in the tabernacle, and Christ ministers in both apartments in the heavenly temple. *Hebrews* 9: 21-24 state that both the tabernacle and vessels were "patterns of things in heaven." Christ's work in the heavenly sanctuary corresponds to that performed by the priests in both apartments of the temple on earth. The yearly work of the priest in the most holy place to cleanse the temple, also known as the Day of Atonement, was a special work. It follows then, that the work of Christ in the second apartment of the heavenly temple must be special. It is a work of like nature, and involves the close of the work as our Great High Priest, and the cleansing of the heavenly sanctuary. [42]

The high priest was required to make solemn preparation and diligently guard himself from contamination while he ministers in the most holy place. While the antitypical atonement is going on in heaven, those who minister in sacred. things must be holy. (www.sdabol.org)

Christ is in heaven, and is officiating as intercessor on behalf of humanity. Through Christ our sins are transferred to the heavenly sanctuary, where He is ministering. Only through the blood of Jesus is the remission of sins possible, no one can go to God except through Christ, He is the Way, the Truth and Door to salvation. The shedding of the blood of animals was just a figure representing what the blood of Jesus means to the sinner. Animal blood could not atone for our sins. Suffice it to say, now that Jesus had given His blood there is no more need for the shedding of animal blood.

Though the slaying of animals could not bring us forgiveness, nor pay for our freedom, these sacrifices had great value to the seeker after forgiveness. The offering made, signified faith in the real sacrifice to come, who was Jesus Himself. It means therefore that those who by faith had engaged in animal sacrifice would have the same interest in Christ's work as those in the post-Calvary era, who come to Him by faith through the observance of the gospel.

In type, the cleansing of the temple by the high priest was the annual closing work of the year's service. He was required to make the most solemn preparation, and diligently guard himself while in the most holy place. In antitype, the cleansing of the sanctuary must be the closing work of Jesus our High Priest, in the tabernacle in heaven. While the antitypical atonement is going on in heaven, those who minister in sacred things must be holy. (*Exodus in Type and Antitype www. sdabol.org*).

> In the type, to cleanse the sanctuary, the high priest entered into the most holy place to minister in the presence of God before the ark of His testament. In antitype, when the time comes for the cleansing of the true sanctuary, our High Priest in like manner, enters into the most holy place once for all to make a final end of His intercessory work in behalf of mankind. [43]

By now, the reader should understand the importance of the sanctuary subject, and appreciate its significance in the plan of salvation. Please note that the whole plan of salvation centers here. When it is done, human probation will be finally closed, and the cases of the saved and lost will be finally decided. Do you see that the cleansing of the sanctuary is a brief and special work? Do you realize that if we can ascertain when the work began we can be assured, based on the signs of the time, that salvation's last mighty hour is upon us? *Revelation* 14:7 says, "Fear God and give glory to Him for the hour of His judgment is come" (*Daniel & Revelation* p. 169).

This is what the prophecy of Daniel 8:14, is about to make known the beginning of the all-important work. "**Unto two thousand three hundred days; then shall the sanctuary be cleansed**." The heavenly sanctuary is where the verdict of all cases will be decided. Because this work concerns every person on planet earth, it follows then that the progress of the work should be of utter importance to humanity. It is to humanity's spiritual benefit to understand and prayerfully consider the importance of these subjects.

Interpretation of the Vision

But I wanted to understand more of what I had seen and to know what it meant. So the One standing on the other side of the Ulai River said to my angel, Gabriel, explain the vision to Daniel and help him understand. Then I realized that the Holy One who spoke was the Son of Man.

[17]So, Gabriel came over to where I was standing, and when he came close, I was so terrified that I fell to my knees, my face on the ground. He said, "Daniel, though you don't understand everything, all you need to know for now is that the vision extends to the time of the end" (*Daniel* 8: 15-18).

Daniel longed to know what the vision meant, so the angel Gabriel came to explain it to him. Daniel was overcome with the majesty of the heavenly messenger, so much so that he fell to the ground. The angel touched him, and helped him to his feet.

After the angel made a general statement that the vision would last to the time of the end, he proceeded to explain it. The ram with two horns, represented the Persian Empire, namely Media and Persia. When these two kingdoms fall, Greece under the leadership of Alexander the Great, (which represented the he goat that had a notable horn) would kill the ram. The prophecy happened exactly as was predicted, but things changed after the premature death of Alexander the Great.

When he died his kingdom was fragmented, but was later consolidated into four divisions headed by his four generals. Alexander was the notable horn of the goat that was broken and four came up in its place, represented the second phase of the goat. However, these horns did not have the strength of the first horn or kingdom, for none of them was as great as Alexander.

Daniel 8: 23-25, explain this further.

> As their kingdom weakens, another kingdom will slowly arise and conquer many kingdoms. After this very bold little king will come and take over Who is full of intrigue even claiming to understand divine mysteries.
> [24] The power of this bold little king will grow stronger and stronger. He will control mighty nations who will wield the sword for him. Through them he will successfully destroy other kings and destroy God's people. [25] He will use cunning and deceit to achieve his ends and will succeed in whatever he does. In his own mind, he will consider himself great. Without warning, he will attack and destroy. He will stand up against the Prince of princes by making claims that belong only to

Him. The kingdom of this bold little king will be destroyed, though not by human hands (*CW*).

This kingdom spoken of, succeeds the four divisions of the goat kingdom. This succeeding kingdom is the same as that spoken of in *Daniel 8:9*.

> Then the wind from the west blew stronger, and out of it came a little horn (that is from one of the four kingdoms) which soon grew bigger and stronger than the other four horns combined. And as it grew, it first pointed south and east, and finally towards the Promised Land.

A King of Fierce Countenance.

Moses spoke of the punishment that should come upon the Jews by this power; he calls it, "a nation of fierce countenance." No other nation appeared in warlike array as the Roman nation did. It was because of the event recorded in *Deuteronomy 28: 49, 50* concerning the transgression of the Jews that they were sold into captivity. Instead of them repenting, they sunk deeper and deeper into sin, and their punishment became more and more severe. The Jews worst time of moral depravation was the time they came under the rule of Roman jurisdiction.

Papal Rome mighty, but not by his own power.

The success of the Romans was largely dependent on the advantage they took when their enemies were divided, and in a significant way with the aid of their allies. In *Ezekiel* 21:31 the Lord told the Jews He would deliver them to men who were "skillful to destroy." This prophecy happened when the Romans at the destruction of Jerusalem destroyed eleven thousand Jews. In addition, Rome was responsible for the death of millions of martyrs.[44]

Through his policy, also he shall cause craft to prosper in his hand. More than any other power, Rome has used craft to bring nations under control. This is true of both pagan and papal Rome. "Thus by peace it destroyed many." The worst of its act was using one of its governors (Pontius Pilate), to condemn the Prince of princes, Jesus Christ, and sentence Him to death. "But he shall be broken without hands." *Daniel* 2:34, says "While you were looking at it, you saw a huge rock break from a mountain without anyone touching it, and strike the statute on his feet of iron and clay, smashing them to pieces." (*CW*).

> This self-operating stone destroys all earthly powers.
> *Daniel* 8: 26, 27 "The vision having to do with the three and a
> half years, each representing a year is true. But for now, you don't
> need to understand more than what I have told you because it
> applies to the time of the end, far in the future. [27] I was so
> overcome by what I had seen that for days afterwards I felt sick.
> Finally, I went back to work to carry on the king's business.
> But, I continued to be amazed at what I had seen in vision and
> wanted desperately to know more of what it meant."

This vision refers to the period of 2300 days. Thinking of the long period of oppression and the calamities to befall his people, Daniel fainted, and was sick for a time. He was surprised at the vision but did not understand it. Without question, Daniel had received just the amount of information he could bear. However, troubled about what he had heard, Daniel began studying the prophecy of Jeremiah which then became clear to him. Exercising faith founded on the sure word of prophecy, Daniel pleaded with the Lord for fulfillment of this promise.

Daniel sought the Lord in earnest. "And I set my face unto the Lord to seek by prayer and supplications, with fasting, and sackcloth, and ashes" (*Daniel* 9:3). He was especially interested in the sanctuary, so he prayed for revelation.

[17] "Now therefore, O our God, hear the prayer of thy servant, and his supplications and cause Thy face to shine upon Thy sanctuary that is desolate, for the Lord's sake."

Isaiah 65: 24 says, "And it shall come to pass, that before they call, I will answer: and while they are yet speaking, I will hear." God made this promise to Isaiah thousands of years ago, and He is still faithful in keeping His promises. Whether the matter is great or small, the reader is encouraged to take it to the Lord in prayer. We have the assurance in God's words that He will hear and answer when we pray. He did just that for Daniel, and He will do it for you and me.

Daniel 9:21 "Gabriel quickly flew to my side to help me. He was the one, who had talked to me before, It was about the time of evening worship when he arrived and helped me to better understand parts of the vision" (*CW*).

An angel flew quickly to Daniel in answer to his prayer to reveal to him:

- the interpretation of the earthly sanctuary
- how it would affect the future
- how it would affect those living in the end time
- scenes of the heavenly sanctuary service.

[22] Daniel, I'm here to tell you what's happening behind the scenes and to help you understand things more clearly. [23] As soon as you started praying, God asked me to come and help you. So now, I'm here to give you more insight into the vision. You are dearly loved by God. So listen carefully to my explanation of how you and your people fit into the vision (*CW*).

The 2300-day period was the only unexplained portion of the vision, so the angel started the interpretation at that point.

[42] Daniel and the Revelation pp.167,168.

[43] Ibid, p.169.

[44] Daniel and the Revelation p. 173.

[45] *Bible Reading* pp., 91.

CHAPTER 23

The Kingdom of God

From the cities and villages, multitudes followed Jesus as He traveled through Galilee healing and teaching. The enthusiasm was always so high, that Jesus had to be careful not to give the Romans the impression that there may likely be an insurrection. This was a special period for the world never before experienced. People who were longing for the redemption of Israel, now was in the presence of their merciful Savior.

Heaven came down to man. Jesus emphasized that, "The time is fulfilled, and the kingdom of God is at hand: repent ye, and believe the gospel." Hence, the gospel message as given by Jesus, was in connection with the prophecies. The "time" which He said was fulfilled, was the same time that was told by the angel to Daniel. The appointed time for Jesus to die for humanity had arrived. Of the **2300**-day prophecy, **70** weeks were to be cut off at the beginning of that period and the Messiah was the focus of that period. A day in prophecy is equivalent to one year. *(Numbers 14:34, Ezekiel 4:6)* It therefore means that seventy weeks or four hundred ninety days, represent four hundred ninety years. **(490** years) In *Hebrews*, the word "determined" translates "to cut," "to cut off." In *Daniel* 9: 24, it is evident that the seventy weeks came from the 2300 days of Daniel 8, and were cut off and allocated to the Jews. Both the 2300 days (period) and the seventy weeks (period) deal with the bringing back of the Jewish people from captivity, and the rebuilding of the temple at Jerusalem that lay in ruins. (See chapter 24).

Daniel 9: 24 "Seventy weeks," said the angel, "are determined upon thy people, and upon thy holy city." This specific period of "seventy weeks," had a significant implication on the people and God's holy city. During this period, some specific occurrences were to take place:

- *To finish the transgression*—the Jewish people were to magnify their iniquity, and they did that, by rejecting and crucifying Jesus.
- *To make an end of sins*—This is that offering made for sin, and this ended with the ultimate offering of Christ on Calvary for the sins of humanity.
- *To make reconciliation for iniquity*—This was done by the sacrificial death of the Son of God on our behalf.
- *To bring in everlasting righteousness*—Jesus manifested in the sinless life He lived. It is the righteousness by which Christ was able to make atonement for sin and is imputed by faith to the penitent believer.
- *To seal up the vision and prophecy*—During this period the prophecy was to be tested, sealed or made sure. This would determine the accuracy of the whole vision. If the events of this prophecy were accurately fulfilled then it is of God and will be accomplished. If the seventy weeks are fulfilled as weeks of years, then the 2300 days of which these are apart, are so many years.
- *To anoint the Most Holy.*—*Daniel* 9:24 speaks of anointing referring to this prophecy. The tabernacle was anointed for the typical service, therefore it is only appropriate for the heavenly sanctuary to be anointed for the antitypical, or real service as Jesus

our Great High Priest enters upon His gracious work of ministry on behalf of sinners (*Hebrews* 8:2).

For more than a century before the birth of Cyrus, God had chosen him to deliver His people from captivity.[45]

Isaiah 44:28 reads, That *says* of Cyrus, "He is my shepherd and shall perform all My pleasure: even saying to Jerusalem, Thou *shall* be built; and to the temple, thy foundations *shall* be laid." (paraphrased).

> Jeremiah also refers to Cyrus as shepherd. *Jeremiah* 25:12, 29.
> And it shall come to pass, when seventy years are accomplished, that I will punish the king of Babylon, that nation, *says* the LORD, for their iniquity, and the land of the Chaldeans, and will make it perpetual desolations. [29] For, lo, I begin to bring evil on the city which is called by My name, and should he, be utterly unpunished? Ye shall not be unpunished: for I will call for a sword upon all the inhabitants of the earth, *says* the LORD of hosts. (emphasis added).

God works in mysterious ways to perform His work, so while the faithful ones in exile were studying the prophecies foretelling their deliverance, He was preparing the hearts of kings to show them favor. Prayer is a very effective and powerful key in the hand of faith to unlock heaven's storehouse of blessings. Daniel though busy, studied and prayed for clarity of the 70 weeks that were cut for the Jews.

Daniel knew that many of God's promises are conditional, and he was wary that the impenitence of the people might postpone the fulfillment of the promise. Furthermore, he did not understand the vision of evening and morning. He prayed and supplicated. If Daniel had handled the unrevealed vision with nonchalance, he might not have been given the rest of the vision, and there is no telling what the outcome would be. Thank

God, Daniel had a relationship with God, and a love for his people, so he prayed, and God answered his prayer.

Dear reader, make prayer your first priority. Before you try anything or anyone, try prayer. In good times and in bad, during sunshine or in the shadow, whether you are having a mountain top experience or you are down in the valley, the advice is the same. Try Jesus. Writer of this song puts it this way,

> Pray when the storm clouds gather o'er head hiding the light from you,
> Filling your heart with darkness and dread,
> Pray till the light shines through.
> Just keep on praying till light shines through
> The Lord will answer; He'll answer you
> God keeps His promise, His word is true,
> Just keep on praying till light shines through.

> Now therefore, our God, the Great, the Mighty, and the Terrible God, who keeps covenant and mercy; let not all the trouble seem little before thee, that hath come upon us, on our kings, on our princes, and our priests, and our prophets, and our fathers, and on all thy people, since the time of the kings of Assyria unto this day.
> (*Nehemiah* 9:32 emphasis added)

God answered Daniel's prayer concerning the repatriation of the Jews as recorded in Ezra, in three ways:

- He stirred up Cyrus in his first year. The decree of Cyrus pertained to the temple only.
- The decree of Darius for the execution of the work, first hindered by Smerdis. Darius gave permission for the continuance of the work.

- In the seventh year of Artexerxes' decree to Ezra 457 B.C., to return and build the temple.[46] This decree therefore, is the one from which the seventy weeks and the 2300 are reckoned.

[46] *Bible Reading p. 92*
[47] Ibid p.93

Other References
Ezra 1: 1-4, 6: 1-12, 7: 1-26.

CHAPTER 24

2300 Days Prophecy

God sometimes uses strange phenomenon and unlikely persons to do His will, as exemplified in the repatriation of the Jews to their homeland. The same nations who had taken them into exile, was now instrumental through their kings to send them home. He caused Cyrus to mandate instructions concerning the building of the temple, and Darius to contribute to the progress of the work. Artaxerxes gave a letter to Ezra giving him permission to restore all the Jewish government. He made it possible for them to enforce their laws, and everyone who wanted to return had the privilege to do so. He also granted the group building materials and goods.

Just as how the prophetic clock had reached the **70** weeks exile of the people of God in Babylon, so it had now reached the time for their return to rebuild the walls and the temple in their homeland. Though Cyrus and Darius were involved in some way for the restoration of the Jews, provision for full restoration was incomplete. However, Artexerxes being the recipient of the initial kings' recommendations, in the seventh year of his reign, was the first to give the Jews full permission to return home, subject to Persian supervision. [48]

(See Chapter 4 for an explanation why Israel was in Babylon).

If the prophecy is to be meaningful, it is important to know when this period of 2300 days/years began. The repatriation and restoration of the people and the temple took place in **457 B.C.**

The seventy weeks period, was divided into three distinct periods. The divisions are as follows:

- **7** Weeks or 49 years—command of Artexerxes.
- **62** Weeks or 434 years—the restoration of Jerusalem.
- **1** Week or (7 years) In the middle of the week allotted to the cutting off Messiah, or His crucifixion.

Total number of Weeks = **70**. Total number of years = **490** years. The Jews had a chance during this time to repent and fulfill their God given mission.

From the above, note that a total of **490** years from the original **2300** years, leaves a remainder of **1810** years; therefore the total of 2300 years would end in 1844. This is the year the prophecy speaks of, "Unto 2300 days then shall the sanctuary be cleansed." [49] (Refer to chapter 20, to remind yourself about the cleansing of the sanctuary).

Please remember, from the prophecy of 2300 days, (years) seventy weeks were cut off or determined for the Jews. Among the things to happen during that time, was the restoration of Jerusalem.

> Know therefore and understand, that from the going forth of the commandment to restore and to build Jerusalem unto Messiah the Prince shall be seven weeks, and three score and two weeks: the streets shall be built again, and the wall, even in troublous times. (*Daniel* 9:25-27).

From the verse, it is clear **69 weeks**, are taken from the **70 weeks**, which ultimately comes from the original **2300-day prophecy**. This **69 weeks** period included the following:

(a) restoring and rebuilding Jerusalem to Messiah the Prince (Jews were to return and rebuild Jerusalem).

(b) rebuilding the street and wall. (Jesus would be crucified in the middle of the week, which is 31/2 years into His ministry. This is half of the seven years remaining from the **70** weeks).

(c) Jesus would be crucified in the middle of the week, which is 3 1/2 years into His ministry.

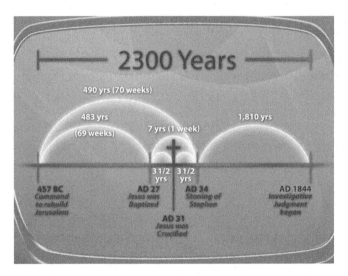

2300 Days Chart 51(a)

From the autumn of **457 B.C.,** the decree that went into effect, **(69 weeks or 483 years)** reached to the baptism of Jesus in **A.D. 27. Sixty-nine** weeks ended in the fall of **A.D.27**, at the baptism of Jesus. The middle of the week or 31/2 years (mentioned above, after His baptism), ended in the spring of **A.D. 31**, when Jesus was crucified. His death brought to an end the sacrifices and oblations of the earthly sanctuary. (*Matthew.* 27: 51,

Mark 15: 38). The other 31/2 years remaining, totaled the end of the **70** weeks/**490** year period, ended in **A.D. 34**. At the expiration of this period of **70** weeks or **490** years, the Jews confirmed their rejection of Christ by the persecution of His disciples, including the stoning of Stephen. From that point on the apostles turned to the Gentiles.[50]

UNTO 2300 DAYS THEN SHALL THE SANCTUARY BE CLEANSED

Unto 2300	Days Then	Shall The	Sanctuary	Be	Cleansed	
BC	BC	AD	AD	AD	AD	AD
457	408	27	31	34	1810	1844

7 weeks	3score & 2 weeks	69 weeks	1 week
49 years	434 years	483 years	7 years

49 years + 434 years + 7 years = 490 years   (2300-490=1810)

A day in prophecy represents a year, therefore 70 weeks would be 70 times 7=490 years, the time determined upon the people.

EVENTS   THAT TOOK PLACE DURING THESE PERIODS

| The comm- and of king Artexerxes king of Per- sia to re- store and build Jeru- salem. 457 B.C. Dan. 9:25 Ezra 6: 1, 6-12 | The recon- struction and resto- ration of the Jeru- salem. This was completed at the end of the first 49 years of the prophecy of Daniel's prediction Dan. 9;25 | Jesus a- nointed with the Holy Spirit at His bap- tism. Matt.3:16 Acts 10:38 From 457 B.C. to Christ the Anointed One, = 483 years. | Messiah cut off in the middle of the week that is 31 A.D. Dan. 9:27 Matt. 27: 50,51 | Stoning of Stephen Gospel goes to the Gen- tiles. Dan,9:24 Acts 2:54, 8;1 From 457 B.C.to this time of the Gentiles = 490 years | The year 1844 is the end of 2300 days/ year pro- phecy, cleansing of the Heavenly Sanctuary, Hour of God's judgment Dan. 8:14 Rev. 14:7 | The three- fold mess- age of Rev. 14:6-12 Heralded to all the world just before Christ's second coming. |

2300 Days Chart 51 (b)

Above Reference Jesus would be crucified in the middle of the week, which is 3 1/2 years into His ministry. [51]

Let the reader note that God's perfect timetable is always reliable. He exalts His words over His name, *(Psalm* 138:2) and it is a fact that He keeps His words. His words are true and faithful. The specifications of every aspect of the prophecy had been without doubt, fulfilled at the appointed time. The work of investigative judgment is on going, since 1844. Based on the prophecy of Daniel, Jesus will be returning with His reward, to give every man according to his work. He that has an ear let him hear. "And, Behold, I come quickly; and my reward is with *Me,* to give everyman according as his work shall be" *(Revelation* 22:12; *emphasis added).*

Let us take a close view of the period **69** weeks or 483 years taken from the **70 weeks** or **490 years.** This sixty-nine weeks, would reach Messiah the Anointed One. His baptism and anointing by the Holy Spirit in **A.D. 27,** was fulfilled to specification. In the middle of the seventieth week, Messiah would be cut off. Three and a half years after His baptism and His public ministry. He was crucified in the year **A.D. 31.** Of the **70** weeks, 3 1/2 years remained for the Jews to do what was expected of them, that of accepting Christ and His mission. Sadly, they did not for in **A.D. 34,** they sealed their rejection of Jesus, by persecuting and killing His disciples, chief of whom was Stephen. This was the year their **70 weeks/ 490 years** allotted to them expired. From 2300 years, 490 years have now expired, leaving a total of 1810 years.[52] (See graphic for confirmation).

Every prophecy was clearly, and obviously fulfilled according to their designated times, except for the cleansing of the sanctuary in 1844. Many thought Jesus would come back to earth in 1844, (at the end of the 2300 day prophecy) to receive His faithful children but that never happened. This event is called "The Great Disappointment." Did that mean God had left His children to wander in darkness as to what the event from that period would be? Certainly not. God would not leave His word to guessing, uncertainty and doubt. Though many had abandoned their former reckoning of the prophetic period, others would not abandon their faith in Jesus, nor renounce points of faith that were sustained by Scriptures and the witness of God's Spirit. They believed that their former interpretations of the Scriptures about the prophecies were correct.

They were also convinced that it was their duty to hold on to the truth already gained, and to continue to pray earnestly and search the Scriptures, to find their mistake. There was no error in their prophetic calculations, so the next decision was to examine closely the subject of the sanctuary.

As these faithful ones searched the Scriptures, they found out that there was no evidence to support the view, that the earth is the sanctuary; and of Jesus coming back to cleanse the sanctuary here in 1844. The location, nature and services of the sanctuary were now clear beyond all questions. (See Appendix H).

Paul the apostle, in the Epistle to the *Hebrews 9: 1-5*, makes it clear that the first covenant dealt with ordinances. Paul is referring to the earthly tabernacle built by Moses at the instruction given to him by God. In verse 11, he said Christ came as a High Priest of good things . . . and more perfect tabernacle, not made with hands . . . In verse 24, he gives a very telling account of the work in which Jesus would engage.

"For Christ is not entered into the holy places made with hands, which are figures of the true; but into heaven itself, now to appear in the presence of God for us." From this account, the early believers would deduce that Jesus would begin His meditorial work in heaven, in 1844.

If you truly want to understand this prophecy, the Holy Spirit is ready and willing to impart knowledge and wisdom in abundance, if you ask. Just think of the difference an illumined mind would make amid the darkness of false theories and teachings.

The Bible is not a fairy tale book with curious signs and symbols, as some would want to have us believe. "All scripture is given by inspiration of God, and is profitable for doctrine, for reproof, for correction, for instruction in righteousness" (*2 Timothy* 3:15).

Temporary Wilderness Sanctuary

As Israel traversed in the wilderness, God wanted to have a place to meet them, so He instructed Moses to make a sanctuary. He said, "Let them make Me a sanctuary that I may dwell among them" (*Exodus* 25; 8). This tabernacle was made of portable material, which was transported by the Israelites during their wilderness journey. The outer court contained the burnt offering, and the other two compartments the holy and the most holy, were separated by a costly beautiful curtain. A similar curtain or veil closed the entrance to the first apartment. In the holy place was the candlestick with its seven lamps, giving light by night and day, the table of shew bread on the north and the veil the golden alter of incense, from which the cloud of fragrance, mingled with the prayers of Israel was ascending daily before God.

In the most holy place was a wooden box overlaid with gold in which were the two tables of stone on which were written the Ten Commandments written by God's own finger. On the top of this box was the mercy seat crafted with exquisite workmanship, and at each end a cherubim facing each other. God's presence was manifested by the cloud of glory between the cherubims.[53]

The cherubims look reverently upon the mercy seat, to indicate the interest with which the heavenly host embraces the work of redemption (*Ibid.*, p. 367). This is a mystery of mercy that angels want to understand. How can God being so just, justify the repenting sinner and Christ the spotless Lamb of God rescues man from the abyss of sin and puts on him

His own robe of righteousness? Paul refers to this structure as man-made, and as the first sanctuary.

Under the Levitical covenant, there were specific rules for worship connected with a fabricated sanctuary (*Hebrews 9:1 CW*). When the time came for the Israelites to move to another location, the portable tabernacle was dismantled and then set up in the new location. However, when they settled in Canaan, this temporary tabernacle was replaced by Solomon's temple, which was a permanent structure.

Solomon's Temple

Solomon's temple had the same proportions, and similar furnishings, as the temporary wilderness temple. This was the same temple destroyed by the Romans in **A.D. 70**, which the returning Jews should rebuild. This was the only fixed sanctuary on record that existed on earth, of which the Bible speaks of the first covenant.

Paul makes mention of a second or new-covenant sanctuary.

The whole point of which I've said is this: our new High Priest is so great that He took His seat at the right hand of the Majesty of heaven and earth.[2] He is serving in the true sanctuary, which is in heaven, set up by God and not by man *Hebrews 8: 1, 2 (CW)*.

Here it is obvious that the sanctuary of the first covenant was erected by man, but the second or new-covenant, was established by the Lord and not man. In the first covenant, the earthly priest performed the sanctuary services, while in the second covenant, Jesus Christ our Great High Priest, ministers at God's right hand. It follows then that if Christ is ministering at the right hand of God, the second sanctuary must be in heaven, and is still in existence. The first, or synthetic, temple erected by Moses in the wilderness, no longer exists. Though the earthly tabernacle was to be a temporary one, Moses was given instructions how to build it. Our God is particular and He is a God of order. He also gave Moses instructions as to how he should organize the work.

> I want you to supervise its construction and see that its furnishings are exactly like the plan I'll show you, which is patterned after things in heaven. My Sanctuary will have its own measurement. A hand's breath is to be added to each cubic, making a Sanctuary cubic twenty-two inches. Be very careful that you make every thing according to the plan, which is patterned after the heavenly Sanctuary, I showed you on the mountain *(Exodus 25: 9, 40 CW)*.

The wilderness sanctuary built by Moses was a copy of the original sanctuary in heaven, in which Jesus now ministers on our behalf. God's Spirit guided the builders of the sanctuary, and everything was done to specification. The splendor of the earthly sanctuary, presented to the people a representation of the glories of the heavenly, where Christ ministers for us before the throne of God, the abiding place of the King of kings, where, . . . "thousand, thousands of angels minister unto Him, and ten thousand times ten thousands stand before Him" *(Daniel 7:10)*.

Important truths were taught in the earthly sanctuary about the heavenly, and the great work carried out for man's redemption. John saw the temple in vision. In it he saw, seven lamps of fire burning before the throne *(Revelation 4:5)*. He saw an angel having a golden censer: and there was given unto him much incense, that he should offer it with the prayers of all saints on the golden alter which was before the throne *(Revelation 8:3)*. Again, "the temple of God was opened" *(Revelation 11:19)*, and he saw the holy of holies, where the ark of His testament was kept. (paraphrased).

Scriptural evidences prove that there is a sanctuary in heaven; Moses built the earthly temple after the pattern of the one in heaven, given to him by God. Paul in (*Hebrews 8; 9*) declares that the pattern was the true sanctuary in heaven. John says he saw it in heaven (*Revelation 4: 8, 12*).

God's throne is established in righteousness and judgment. The law, which is the rule of right by which all humankind is tested, is situated in the ark in the most holy place. On top of the ark, which contains the tables of the law, is the mercy seat, before which Christ pleads His blood for sinners. Here justice and mercy are united in the plan of redemption.

> Zechariah gives a beautiful description of Jesus as the Branch. Tell him that this is what the Lord Almighty says, "The One who is called the Branch will spring forth from the house of David and will come and glorify the temple.
>
> 12 He will come and build a spiritual temple of the Lord and will be enthroned as Israel's rightful King.
> With majesty He will govern His people and will serve as High Priest, carrying out God's plan to rescue man from sin as agreed between the Father and the Son in heaven's council of Peace" *Zechariah 6:12, 13 (CW)*.

The references to Jesus "glorifying the Temple," "building spiritual temple," being "enthroned as Israel's rightful King," and serves as "High Priest," strongly suggest that Jesus is an integral part of the ministry of the temple. It has to be either the earthly temple, which no longer exists, or the heavenly, which is current. Let us take a close look at why the temple referred to, could not be the earthly, hence has to be the heavenly.

> (*Hebrews 8: 1, 2*) The whole point of what I've said is this: our new High Priest is so great, that He took His seat at the right hand of the Majesty of heaven and earth. 2 He is serving in the

true Sanctuary, which is in heaven, set up by God and not by man.

(Hebrews 9: 24) This is why Christ, who is the better sacrifice, did not stay here to minister in the man-made Sanctuary on earth, which is only a copy of the true one in heaven, but entered heaven itself to appear in the presence of God on our behalf, who is not confined to the Most Holy Place. Paul and John also give vivid accounts of Jesus and redemption . . .

20 To use another analogy, you are like living stones of a beautiful temple carefully securely laid on the foundations of the apostle and prophets, who, in turn, are cemented to Jesus Christ, the great Cornerstone.

21All these stones are joined together into a beautiful, holy temple, being aligned on Christ and raised up to the glory of God. 22And in Christ you too, together with us, are part of this growing temple, in which God through the Holy Spirit, lives" *(Ephesians 2:20-22 CW).*

"He shall build the temple of the Lord," By His sacrifice and meditation, Christ is both the foundation and the builder of the Church of God. Paul refers to Him as "the Chief Cornerstone."

And from Jesus Christ, who is the faithful witness, and the first begotten of the dead and the prince of the kings of the earth. Unto *Him* that loved us, and washed us from our sin in *His* own blood, And hath made us kings and priests unto God and *His* Father. to *Him* be glory and dominion forever and ever. Amen *(Revelation 1: 5, 6).*

The work in heaven could not begin until after Christ offering for sin on the cross (*Heb. 9:25, 26*). He is now our Mediator, or High Priest in the heavenly sanctuary, engaged in the cleansing of the heavenly sanctuary, since 1844 (*Daniel 8:14*). When this work is finished, all the people of God will be ready for His appearing. All their sins would have been forgiven, and placed on Satan the originator of sin. Satan, will bear the responsibility for their sins. (See Chapter 21 for the typical scapegoat).[54]

My dear readers, I know that for some, this is brand new information. One thing I would advise you not to do is down play the significance, of this revelation. Would you treat the news of an eminent tsunami or violent tornado lightly? I guess not. I tell you the deluge is coming, but you do not have to fear, if you open your hearts to these messages and warnings, God will care for His own. Now is the time to make your calling and election sure (*2 Peter 1: 10*).

This very important pronouncement made by the angel to Daniel, **"Unto two thousand and three hundred days: then shall the sanctuary be cleansed,"** is now explained. I hope that each reader has found the meaning of the cleansing of the sanctuary and its application understandable. Please understand that some events are still in the process of completion.

> The heavenly sanctuary is the one in which the decision of all cases is to be rendered. The progress of the work there should be the special concern of mankind. If people understood the bearing of these subjects on their eternal interest, they would give them their most careful and prayerful study.[55]

Summary of the important and solemn positions brought forward:

- The sanctuary of the Christian Era is the tabernacle of God in heaven.
- It is the house not made with hands.
- Jesus ministers in this sanctuary on behalf of penitent sinners.
- It is where the "counsel of peace" prevails between God and His Son Jesus Christ, in the work of the salvation for sinful men. (*Zechariah* 6:13; *Psalm* 85:10).
- Cleansing of the sanctuary involves the removal of sin from it.
- The cleansing of the temple is the final act of the ministration performed in it.
- The work of salvation now centers in the sanctuary.

When the cleansing of the sanctuary is completed, it means the :

- The great plan of salvation to redeem man is finally terminated.
- Mercy no longer pleads, and the voice is heard from heaven to say, "It is done" *(Revelation 16:17)*.

After this call there will be no more forgiveness of sins, whatever state the inhabitants of the earth is in at that time, will determine where they will spend eternity. The righteous will be rewarded with eternal life, and the wicked to everlasting death. These words are true, this earth will have no security, at the coming of Christ, no money, education, or fame will be able to secure your safety if your life is not hid with Christ in God.

There will be only two classes of people when Jesus comes, those who obeyed Him and those who disobeyed Him. He will say well done to the obedient, but to the disobedient, he will say depart. Many will confess at that time but it will be eternally too late. He invites you to come now while the door of mercy is still ajar.

[48] Daniel and the Revelation p.193.

[49] Ibid, p.199.

50   Great Controversy p.369.

51   (a) www.Goodsalt.com

51   (b) Daniel and the Revelation

52   Great Controversy p.363/Daniel and the Revelation p.189.

53   Great Controversy p.367.

54   Ibid, p.373.

55   Daniel and the Revelation pp.169,170.

CHAPTER 25

The Solemn Judgment Hour

From our study we can conclude that the long prophetic period, which was to end at the beginning of the final work of the cleansing of the heavenly sanctuary, ended in 1844. Since then the work of man's salvation has been going forward. This work involves an examination of every man's character, as recorded in the books of heaven. All deeds are recorded in those books (*Revelation* 22: 12). Those who would have been worthy are those whose sins are remitted.

Each one receives a reward according to the deeds done in the body (*2 Corinthians* 5:10: *Revelation* 22: 12). Confessed and forgiven sins have no power over the sinner. The judgment hour message is depicted as angels flying. It would seem that this judgment message is very important and urgent; hence, symbolically angels in flight are taking it.

> Then the scene changed back to the final events on earth, and
> I saw an angel flying high in the air, proclaiming one last time
> the eternal gospel to every nation, tribe, language and people.

⁷ He called out in a loud voice for all to hear, saying, "Honor God and glorify His name, for the time has come for His judgment to begin. Worship Him who created the heavens, and the earth, and the springs of water" (*Revelation* 14: 6, 7).

The message is to be preached to every nation, kindred, tongue and people. Since angels deliver their messages through human, it would mean that this message would be delivered by a great religious movement who would give to men the judgment hour message. God's judgment is eminent, so the angels say, "Fear God and give glory to Him; for the hour of His judgment is come." Judgment is not future anymore it is here. We should worship Him who made heaven and earth, the sea, and every water fountain.

In these days, many doctrinal voices are calling from every direction claiming to be true; the multiplicity of voices leave many people confused as to what to believe. Is it possible for any one to determine who is speaking the truth? Difficult as this may seem, the answer is "yes" The gospel is about the good news of Jesus Christ. The Bible contains the good news about Jesus from Genesis to Revelation. Our belief system should be based on the teachings of the Bible, no other source. If anyone claims to be a true follower of Jesus, what he /she believes should be supported by the Bible, sola scriptura.

Let us look at the cross section of Bible references to discover the truth. There is only one gospel, first spoken of in Genesis 3:15, where God promised Adam after he sinned, that the seed of the woman would crush the head of the serpent. Abraham knew about it *(Galatians* 3:8) and the children of Israel (*Hebrews* 4: 1, 2) heard it anew in succeeding generations. The gospel fulfills the needs of every crisis that the world has and will ever see. (See also *Romans* 16:20, *Revelation* 12:7, *John* 8:44, *Acts* 13:10, 1*John* 3:8, *Isaiah* 7:14, *Luke* 1:31,34, 35, 1*Corinthians* 16:23).

The books of Daniel and Revelation are the prophetic books of the Bible. How is this so? They contain prophetic predictions, and unlike history, are written in advance of their occurrences. Since prophets are men, can any one be a prophet?

Any one can use logical calculations to predict future occurrences, which sometimes happen, but to say the fulfillment of a particular prediction, speculation or calculation, is enough to determine it was prophetic, would be gullible.

On the contrary, when the Bible prophecy predicts an event, it is always accurate, even though the predictions may sometimes be hundreds of years before they happen. As for example, the 2300 days prophecy of Daniel was predicted "Before Christ," and now even thousands of years after Christ's ascension, parts continue to come to pass and will continue to the end of time. How is it so? Because the prophecies of the Bible are, God inspired.

That is what prophecy is about, the foretelling of specific events a long time before they occur. It is also evident, that these books (mentioned above) contain many symbols that have meanings dealing with the predictions of these prophets. As for example, In Daniel 2, Nebuchadnezzar the king of Babylon had a dream about an image. The head of the image was made of gold, representing the king of Babylon. The breast and arms of silver was Medo Persia, the belly and thighs made of brass stood for Greece, and the legs of iron represented Rome. The feet and toes were a combination of iron and clay represented the divided kingdoms of Europe *(Daniel* 2: 31-43). "The barbarian tribes that overran the Roman Empire formed the kingdoms which developed into the nations of modern Europe"(Bible Readings p. 28).

John the Baptist proclaimed that the kingdom of heaven is at hand *(Matthew* 3: 1, 2) and he was the one who prepared the way for the first advent *(John* 1: 22, 23). Close to the second coming of Christ, a worldwide announcement of the preaching of the everlasting gospel fit for the need of the hour will be made. This message found in *Revelation* 14: 6-12. is delivered by three angels.

The first: (Verses 6, 7) has the everlasting gospel to preach to all of earth's inhabitants. The warning is to fear God, and give Him glory, for the hour of His judgment hour is come and to worship Him the Maker of heaven, earth, the sea, and the fountains of waters.

The second angel, verse 8, pronounced the fall of Babylon. According to *Isaiah* 21:9, Babylon is not only fallen, but all her graven images of her gods, are also broken. "Graven images" and "gods" do imply a violation of the first and second commandments *(Exodus* 20: 3-6).

When John the writer of Revelation spoke about the fall of Babylon, the literal Babylon of Nebuchadnezzar was already in ruins. Therefore, it is safe to conclude he was not speaking of the physical Babylon, but spiritual Babylon. Further proof concurs, verse 8 implies the reason Babylon is fallen, is that she made all nations drink of the wine of her fornication. The truth is, all nations cannot fit in physical Babylon, so the reference is not to physical Babylon.

The prophet Isaiah in chapter 13 verses 19-22, give a graphic description of the fate of this once impressive kingdom. They did not honor God, instead they indulged in various forms of idolatry and praised the gods of wood and stone.

> The Babylonian name Bab-ilu (Babel), or (Babylon) meant "gates of the gods," but the Hebrews derogatorily associated it with balal, a word in their language, meaning "to confuse" *(see on Gen. 11:9).* The rulers of Babylon doubtless called their city the "gate" of the gods in the sense that they chose to think of it as the place where the gods consorted with men, to order the affairs of earth. *(see on Judges 9:35; Ruth 4:1;1Kings 22:10;Jer.22:3).* The name thus seem to have reflected the claim of the Babylonian kings that they had been commissioned to rule the world by divine mandate . . .
> Bible Commentary Vol., 7, p 828, 829.

Other References
(*Acts* 3:16; *Isa.* 47:1; *Jer.* 25:12, 50; *Ezek.* 26: 13; *Rev.* 16:12, 16).

The third angel verses 9-11 in a loud voice warned, if any man worship the beast and his image, and receive his mark in the forehead or in the hand, the same shall drink of the wine of the wrath of God, which is poured out unmixed into His cup of indignation . . . This will be the fate of anyone who instead of worshipping God, worships false gods. Conversely, those who heed the warning are described as patience of the saints, and those who keep the commandments of God, and the faith of Jesus Verse 12 (paraphrased).

> Speaking of Rome as a "wicked city" that loves "magic," indulges in "adulteries," and has a "bloodthirsty heart and a godless mind," and observing that "many faithful saints of the Hebrews have perished" because of her, the writer, predicts her eventual desolation: in widowhood, she shall sit beside thy banks . . . *(S.D.A. Bible Commentary p.830).*
> (R.H. Charles, *The Apocrypha and Pseudepigrapha of the Old Testament Vol., p.200 cf. Re. 18:5-8).*

In John's day, the literal ancient city of which Nebuchadnezzar was king, was already in ruins (See *Isaiah* 13:19).

Bab-ilu in Babylonian means (Babel or Babylon) meant "gate of the gods." The Hebrews word for Babel is balal meaning, "to confuse."

(Genesis 11:9) The Babylonians called their city the "gate" which means they chose to think of it as the place where the gods associated with men to rule the affairs of earth.

(Judges 9:35, *Ruth* 4:1, *I Kings* 22:10, *Jeremiah* 22:3)

This claim seems to coincide with the Babylonian kings that they had been commissioned to rule the world by divine mandate (see on Gen. 11:4).

Who or What is Babylon?

The founder of Babylon was Nimrod *(Genesis* 10:10, 11: 1-9). From the very start, the city was a sign of rebellion against and disbelief in God. The reason behind building the city, was in defiance of the authority of God *(Genesis* 4-9). Its towers were a memento of their apostasy, and a citadel of rebellion against God. Isaiah alludes that Lucifer is the invisible *king of Babylon (Isaiah 14:4).*

Although God allowed Israel to be captured and held in Babylon, their demise was not intended to be for an indefinite period. God's punishment is always tempered with mercy. (However, this does not give us the right and freedom to sin at will, because one day might be one day too many for someone).

A happy band of people left Egypt on their way to freedom. Their initial response to freedom was pure joy. Similar to the joy for freedom from Egypt and physical Babylon, He wants us to experience joy and freedom from spiritual Babylon.

When the Lord does this, the people will sing of their release and freedom from their captors in Babylon. They will sing to the Lord and say," The king of Babylon has fallen! Our oppression has ended! We are free! The great city rules us no more!" it would seem Satan has designed that he would make Babylon the center and agency of his plans to control the human race. Throughout the Old Testament, the two cities represent the working of good and evil. The builders of Babylon had intended to establish a government outside of God's will, and had they succeeded they would banish righteousness from the earth, but God stepped in and stopped it. He destroyed the tower and scattered the builders *(Ibid.,* p.829; *Genesis* 11: 7, 8).

Following that, there was a period of short-lived success, followed by a long period of decline and humiliation meted out to them by other nations.

(Isaiah 21:1-17) describe it as a burden.

Over the centuries after Babylon was taken over by the Medes and Persians, the city gradually lost more and more of its importance, and eventually towards the close of the 1st century A.D., it ceased to exist, and would never be rebuilt (*Isaiah* 13:19-21). Close to this period, Christians were already referring to the city and empire of Rome as "Babylon" (*1 Peter* 5: 13) Once again, the Christians were in exile, this time under the merciless hand of Rome.

Since the fall of Babylon, Satan has used Romanism (known by some as modern Babylon) to counterfeit God's plans. Satan has made many attempts from one world power to another to control the world, but as many times, God has intervened to prevent this. The almost successful one has been the papal apostasy of the Middle Age (*Daniel* 7:25). Even this however, has not been a total success (*Revelation* 12, 5, 16). The nations have never been able to cleave together (*Daniel* 2: 43).

The cryptic description of the city of Rome is prevalent in both Jewish and Christian literature. An example of this is found in Book V the *Sibylline Oracles* a pseudepigraphical Jewish production, less than one hundred fifty years after Jesus, (Vol. V, p. 89) gives what could be a prophecy of the fate of Rome that closely fits the description of that of mystical Babylon in the Revelation.

It describes Rome, as a "wicked city" that loves "magic," indulges in "adulteries," and has a "bloodthirsty heart and a godless mind," and allowing many faithful Hebrew saints to perish. Her desolation is certain, according to the writer. "In widowhood *shall* thou sit beside thy banks . . . But thou hast said, I am unique, and none shall bring ruin on me. But now God . . . shall destroy you and all of *yours*." (vs. 37-74; R. H. Charles, *The Apocrypha Pseudepigrapha of the Old Testament*, vol. 2, p. 400; cf. Rev. 18: 5-8). (*Bible Commentary* Vol., 7, p. 830).

One of those who lived close to the second century, Tertullian by name, purports the fact that Babylon in the Apocalypse refers to the capital city of imperial Rome. *(Against Marcion* iii. 13; *Answer to the Jews* 9; see also Iranaeus *against Heresies* v.26 1).

> Both literal and mystical Babylon have been known as enemies of God's truth and people. The name mystical Babylon is symbolic of all apostate religious organizations and their leadership, from the days of ancient Babylon to the end of time. Along with those references to Babylon in Revelation, many Old Testament passages record the sins and fate of literal Babylon *(Isaiah* 47:1; *Jeremiah* 27:12;50:1; *Ezekiel* 23: 17-23; *Jeremiah* 50: 14; Nahum: 3: 4; *Isaiah* 21: 9).

Revelation 12 refers to the church as a woman. The pure woman represents the pure church and the corrupt woman the corrupt or apostate church. The impure woman is also described as the mother of harlots (see on *Revelation* 17). Babylon is not confined to one ecclesiastical body, but is made up of many bodies. It represents the entire corrupt, or apostate churches on planet earth. Please note that the members of these bodies are not Babylon, but are referred to as "waters" as, described in Revelation 17:15.

The call to these people is to come out of Babylon, or false worship *(Rev.* 18:5). Babylon has made all nations drunken with the wine of her false doctrines. Over the years many of these false churches have zealously opposed those who dare differ from their doctrine/traditions. Babylon is therefore qualified as the universal worldly church. "Babylon the great" in the book of Revelation refers to the united apostate religions at the close of time *(Revelation* 14:8; 16:13, 14; 18:24). God calls His people to come out of Babylon, because she is fallen due to her increasing sinfulness, which includes:

- Denying through Immaculate Conception that God in Christ dwelt in human flesh
- Setting aside the mediation of Christ
- Substituting the earthly priesthood for the priesthood of Christ
- Making salvation contingent on confessing to mortal man, thus separating the sinner from Jesus, his only source of forgiveness
- Substituting the doctrine of salvation by works in place of salvation by faith calling it heresy.
  Treasures of Life pp.601,602

They also believe in the natural immortality of the soul, which nullifies the teaching of the Bible on the resurrection and judgment, thus opening the door to spiritism. From this come the evil doctrines of, prayers and baptisms for the dead, purgatory, reward at death, conscious state of the dead, eternal torment mariology, and universal salvation.

In addition, they teach that dead saints become disembodied spirits and find their inheritance far away in indefinable regions. Also that the coming of Jesus is not literal, and that the millennium is a thousand years of peace, prosperity and righteousness before Christ comes.

God's call to His people is to separate themselves from Babylon's false, teachings and beliefs, so they will not share in her downfall. The third angel of Revelation 14:9,10, say, those who worship the beast and his image . . . will share in his punishment.

This chapter of Revelation refers to Babylon as "great," because it deals specifically with Satan's last great effort to secure the allegiance of the human race through religion or worship.

> *The name mystical Babylon is symbolic of all apostate religious organizations and their leadership, from the days of ancient Babylon to the end of time.*

The threefold religious union of the papacy, spiritism, and apostate Protestantism, (*Bible Readings* p. 129) is also known as "Babylon the Great." (*Revelation* 16: 13, 18, 19; *Daniel* 4: 30, *Zechariah* 10: 2, 3; 11: 3-9). Remember that "Babylon" refers to the organization and their leaders, and not to the members who are known as "many waters" (*Revelation* 17: 15) also as the inhabitants of the earth.

Revelation 17: 2, 6 speak of the intoxication of Babylon, and this is not with literal wine, but of the blood of the saints, martyrs of Jesus.

- The dragon represents *Paganism*
- The beast represents the *Papacy*
- The false prophets represents *apostate Protestantism*

These are the three great religious apostates since the flood. (*Revelation* 16:13,14).

"And in her was found the blood of the prophets, and of saints, and of all that were slain upon the earth (*Revelation* 18:24).

Babylon has done it before and will do it again. She is utterly drunk with past success of persecuting the saints and according to *Daniel* 7:25, she will wear out the saints of the Most High.

Take a close look at the capabilities and objectives of Babylon, and compare the account in the two prophetic books of Daniel in the Old Testament and Revelation in the New Testament.

Take a keen look into prophecy, this is for real. Your decision can shape your destiny.

MYSTICAL BABYLON	
Mystical Babylon in the Revelation	Old Testament Parallels
HER IDENTITY AND CHARACTER	
1 Meaning of the name. "Upon her forehead was a name written, Mystery Babylon the great" (17:15) "What city is like unto this great city!" (18:18; 17:5).	1. "There is the name of it called Babel" (*Gen.* 11:9)" Great Babylon" (*Dan.* 4:30; 7:20). "His look was more stout than his fellows" (*Ezek* 26:17; 27: 32).
2 An apostate organization "The great whore" "fornication" "a woman" "mother of harlots and abominations of the earth"17:1-5 cf.14:8,17:6	2. "The lady of the kingdoms" (*Isa.* 47:3). The Babylonians . . . defiled her with their whoredoms
3. *"Wholly corrupt in Character"* "Babylon the great is fallen, and is become the habitation of devils and the hold of every unclean and hateful bird" (18:2)s.	3 "Babylon is fallen, is fallen" (*Isa.* 21: 9) "Babylon *has* sinned against the Lord" (*Jer.* 50:14).

4 *Marked by luxury and pride* "She *has* glorified herself and lived deliciously" "was clothed in fine linen, and purple, and scarlet, and decked with gold, and precious stones, and pearls" (18 :7).	4 "Babylon the glory of kingdoms, the beauty of the Chaldees' excellency" (*Isa* 13:9). "Tender and delicate, given to pleasure" . . . (*Isa.* 47: 1, 8).
5. *Her Counterpart* "That great city of the holy Jerusalem" (21: 10).	5 "The Lord . . . shall choose Jerusalem" (Zech. 2:12). They shall call Jerusalem the throne of the Lord. (Jer. 3:17)

HER AMBITIONS AND OBJECTIVES

6. *To rule the world* "She *says* in her heart, I sit a queen, and am no widow" (18: 7) . . . "makes war with the Lamb" (17;18).	6 "Thou [Babylon] *says,* I shall be a lady forever . . . I shall not sit a widow, neither shall I know the loss of children" (*Isa* 47 :7, 8).
7. *To annihilate the saints* "I saw the woman drunken with the blood of the saints, and with the blood of the martyrs of Jesus"	7. "Babylon *has* caused the slain of Israel to fall" (Jer. 51: 49). *"You* showed them no mercy" (Isa. 47:6).

HER ACCOMPLICES

8. *Demonic spirits* "Babylon is become the habitation of devils" (18: 2). "Three unclean spirits" "the spirits of devils" (16 : 13, 14).	**8.** "The king of Babylon" "Lucifer" (*Isa.* 14 :4, 12; see *Ezek.* 28 :12).
9. *The great powers of earth* A scarlet colored beast (17: 3) "The beast that was, and is not, and yet is" (17: 8, 11).	**9** "Like a lion . . . with eagle's wings" (*Dan.* 7: 4 ; *Jer.* 51 : 25).
10. *All nations* "The ten horns . . . . are ten kings who . . . receive power as kings one hour with the beast" (17: 12) "The kings of the earth (16:14) "These have one mind [and] agree" (17:13, 17).	**10.** "The ten horns" (*Dan* 7 :7). Compare Dan. 2: 43. See on Rev. 17:12.
11. Other apostate religious *Organizations* "Harlots" (17 :5.) "The false prophet"(19 : 20; 20 :10). "An image to the beast, which had the wound by a sword and did live" (13:14).	**11.** See No. 2

12. *The leaders of earth* "Thy merchants were the great men of the earth" (18 : 23).	**12.** "The astrologers, and stargazers, the monthly prognosticators" . . ." the honorable of the earth" (*Isa.* 23:8).
13. *The peoples of the earth* "All nations" (14 : 8; 18 : 3.)	**13** "All the kingdoms of the world upon the face of the earth" (*Isa* 23:17).

HER STRATEGY

14. Universal religio-political union "Sit upon a scarlet *colored*". . . "on which the woman *sits*" (18: 9). "The kings of the earth . . . have committed fornication and lived deliciously with her" (17: 2). "Receive power as king one hour with the beast. "These . . . shall give their power and strength unto the beast" (17 : 12,13).	**14** "[Tyre] shall turn to her hire and shall commit fornication with all the kingdoms of the world upon the face of the earth" (*Isa.* 23 : 17).
15 *Her policy and teachings* "A golden cup in her hand full of abominations and filthiness of her fornication" (17: 4). 'She made all nations drink of the wine of the wrath of her fornication" (14:8). "Did corrupt the earth with her fornication "(19 :2).	**15** "Babylon has been a golden cup in the Lord's hand, and made all the earth drunken: the nations have drunken of her wine; therefore the nations are mad" (*Jer.* 51: 7).

179

16 *Satanic Miracles: deceptions* "The spirits of devils working miracles" (16:14). "By sorceries were all nations deceived" (18: 23). "Great wonders" "miracles" (13:13, 14). "Merchandise" (18:11).	**16**. "The multitude of thy [Babylon] sorceries" "the great abundance of thy enchantments" (*Isa.* 47 : 9). With a few exceptions, the long list of Revelation 18:12, 13 are duplicated in Ezek. 27.
17 *Absolute control of men's minds* "*Sits* upon many waters" (that is)	**17** "*Dwells* upon many waters" (*Jer.* 51:13) "All peoples, nations, and languages, trembled and feared before him" (*Dan* 5: 19).

HER FATE

18. *God arraigns Babylon* "It is done" Great Babylon came in remembrance before God, to give unto the wine of the fierceness of his wrath" (16, 17, 19).	**18** "I have taken out of thine [Israel's] the cup of trembling . . . but I will put it into the hand of them that afflict thee" (*Isa* 51:22, 23)." I will punish the king of Babylon . . . God *has* numbered *your* kingdom, and finished it . . . "*You* are weighed in the balances and . . . found wanting" (*Dan.* 5: 26, 27).

19 *Her accomplices turn against her* "God *has* put in their hearts to fulfill His will, and to agree and give their kingdoms unto the beast . . . (17:17)." "These have one mind" (17:13). "Gathered the kings of the earth 'to the battle of the great day of God Almighty" (16: 14). "These shall make war with the Lamb, and the Lamb shall overcome them" "The ten horns" and "the beast . . . shall hate the whore . . . and shall eat her flesh and burn her with fire" (17: 16)	**19**: "I will bring upon that land [Babylon] all my words which I have pronounced against it" (*Jer.* 25:13). "Blow the trumpet among the nations, prepare the nations against her" (*Jer.* 51: 27, 29). "I will raise and cause to come up against Babylon an assembly of great nations" (*Jer.* 50: 9). "I will kindle a fire in her cities" (*Jer.* 50; 32).
20. *Her annihilation is absolute* "A mighty angel took up a stone like a great mill stone and cast it into the sea saying, Thus with violence shall that great city Babylon be thrown down, and shall be found no more at all. (18:21).	**20** "The sea is come up upon Babylon: . . . thus shall Babylon sink, and shall not rise from the evil, that I will bring upon her" (*Jer.* 51; 42, 63, 64) 'Two things shall come to *you* in one day, the loss of children, and widowhood' "None shall save *you*" (*Isa.* 47; 9, 11, 13). "Thy kingdom is divided" (Dan. 5: 28). "Babylon is taken" "make her land desolate and none shall dwell therein" (*Jer.* 50: 2, 3, 13, 40)

21. *"Her punishment appropriate to her crimes* "Reward her even as she rewarded you, and double unto her double according to her work ... how much she *has* glorified herself, and lived deliciously, so much torment and sorrow give her" (18 :6, 7).	21 "I will recompense them according to their deeds and according to the works of their own hands" (*Jer.* 25:14). "I will render unto Babylon . . . all their evil that they have done in Zion" (*Jer.* 51: 24) "As she *has* done do unto her." (*Jer.* 50: 15, 29).
22. *Her accomplices lament her* "The kings of the earth . . . shall bewail her, and lament for her, when they shall see the smoke of her burning." (18: 9, 10).	22 "Howl for her [Babylon]" (Jer. 51:8) "Let now the astrologers, the stargazers, the monthly prognosticators, stand up ... The fire shall burn them ... they shall wander every one to his quarter' (*Isa.* 47: 13-15). "Every one ...shall be astonished, and hiss at all her plagues" (*Jer.* 50 : 13) Compare Ezek 26:16, 17; 27: 29-32, 36; 28:19
23. *Her accomplices are destroyed* "The cities of the nations fell" (16: 19). "The beast . . . shall go into perdition" (17: 8). " Both the beast and the false prophets were cast alive into a lake of fire burning with brimstone" (19 :20)	23 "I will gather all nations against Jerusalem to battle" (*Zech.* 14: 2, Joel 3: 2) .... "And the slain of the Lord shall be at that day from one end of the earth even unto the other end of the earth" (*Jer.* 25: 31, 33). "At Babylon shall fall the slain of the earth" (*Jer.* 51: 49).

24. *A song of victory over Babylon* "He *has* avenged the blood of His servants at her hands" (19: 2). "Rejoice over her thou heaven and ye holy apostle and prophets" (18: 20).	**24** "This is the time of the Lord's vengeance upon [Babylon]" "The Lord *has* spoiled Babylon" (*Jer.* 51:6, 55). "Then the heaven and the earth, and all that is therein, shall sing for Babylon: for the spoilers shall come unto her" (*Jer.* 51: 48).

GOD'S WARNING TO HIS PEOPLE

25 *Come out of Babylon* "Another angel" came down from heaven having great power; and the earth was lightened with his glory. And he cried mightily with a strong voice" (18:1, 2) "Come out of her my people, that ye be not partakers of her sins, and that ye receive not of her plagues"(18:4).	**25.** "Deliver thyself O Zion that *dwells* with Babylon" *Zech.* 2: 7). "Flee out of the . . . of Babylon, and deliver every man his soul; be not cut off in her iniquity." (*Jer.* 51: 6, 45). "My people ego ye out of the midst of her, and deliver ye every man his soul from the fierce anger of the Lord" (*Jer.*51:6,45 cf. *Isa.* 48:20; 52:11; *Jer.*50:8; 51:9).

S.D. A Bible Commentary (Vol. 7 p. 867-869).

Matthew 24: 21 says," For then shall be great tribulation, such as was not since the beginning of the world to this time, no, or ever shall be."

The good news however, is that Babylon's tyranny will come to an end, and sin and sinners will be forever gone. Babylon will fall.

CHAPTER 26

The Fall of Babylon

Obedient children, most often escape the punishment the disobedient receive. In the judgment, it will not only be a good feeling to escape punishment, but to enjoy all the provisions Jesus has prepared for the obedient.

Maybe someone reading this book would have been hearing for the first time about the judgment, and sanctuary. Not to worry, God knew this and He has made provision for these dear ones. Paul says:

"He has overlooked our past ignorance. He expects people everywhere to turn to Him and change their ways." My friend Jesus promises to come back and receive those who love and obey Him. He will not hold past confessed wrongs against you. Whatever the past, He will forgive if you but ask. "He has fixed a day in time when He will judge the world by a Man of His own choosing. Proof of this is that He has already raised Him from the dead" *(Acts 17: 30, 31)*. That day of judgment will not have any adverse effect on you if you give Him your heart now, rather it will be a day of rejoicing for the Judge will be your Brother and Friend.

The reader should note that knowledge is power, therefore it is good to know, but with knowledge comes responsibility. God overlooked, or winked before exposure to knowledge, but now He expects the knowledgeable to act on imparted knowledge.

There is no room for excuse of ignorance, because lets face it, many sacrifice life, health, and well-being at the altar of "gain." There is no telling what some folks would do just to be rich. The story is told of a desert traveler, who was promised all the land his feet would tred upon for the entire day. He started his journey very excited, at the prospect of being rich at the end of the day. He started out with brisk steps, but as the desert sun took its toll on his body, his steps became slower and painful. He had consumed most of his water by mid-day, but he comforted himself that evening was coming, and it would be cooler soon. His exhausted body was saying "enough," but he wanted to take just a few more steps, before night-fall and that would be enough for him. One last painful step and "thud," he fell unconscious to the ground. He had exchanged life for riches, which he never received anyway.

Jesus asked His hearers a question, and He is asking the same question to every reader: "What profit is there in gaining the whole world and all the good things of this life if it causes you to lose your own soul?" What can a man give in exchange for his soul?" *(Mark* 8: 36, 37).

Eternal life is far more valuable than temporary treasure. He knows our very thoughts. He knows the secret desires to follow Him, and He sees the fear of the unknown, but He wants me to tell you, you need not fear. When the journey gets too dangerous, He will lift you up.

The wise man Solomon says: "One day He will judge everything we have done in this life, including every secret thing, whether it was good or bad" *(Ecclesiastes* 12:14).

Here we are of men most privileged to be alive when this last great and most solemn crisis in the history of our race is about to be culminated.

Signs of the time should defy any doubt that we are living in the time when the second advent will be realized.

In *Matthew* 24, Jesus enumerated the events that would take place just before His coming, just before human probation is closed, and His pronouncement, "It is Finished," ends the probationary period. The plan of salvation is still available for anyone who answers His call to repent. Are you willing to answer the most important call ever?

This is not about how you were reared, or what tradition teaches, or yet, who may mock, and make fun of you. It is about your destiny, your responsibility, your salvation. Do not be too busy, too proud, or drunken with the cares and pleasures of this world, to surrender your life in true and full obedience to God. The true test of obedience and faithfulness is "Thus says the Lord." If the Bible does not teach it, it is not of the Lord, and it does not matter how much it is dressed up. Jesus will not accept it.

After all is said and done, there is only one thing that really matters: Reverence our heavenly Father and do what He says. the only thing that has meaning and lasts. So love God and keep His commandments. He loves you and has told you all you need to know (*Ecclesiastes 12*: 13).

Salvation comes through Christ alone He paid the ultimate price for sin by His death on the cross. Through His atoning sacrifice, He has prepared a way for everyone to escape eternal death. View the all-important question:

How shall we escape, if we neglect so great salvation; which at first began to be spoken by the Lord, and was confirmed unto us by them that heard *Him? (Hebrews* 2: 3 paraphrased).

It is hoped that the reader will give serious thoughts to answering the invitation of Jesus, "to come just as you are," He will not turn you away. It does not matter to Him how far you have sunken, the past will not be a factor if your present is surrendered to Him. Do it now, not tomorrow, for tomorrow is a promissory note and no one knows what the next minute holds. Friends, today is the day of salvation. He is at the door knocking, "Will you let Him in?"

Make Jesus the center of your joy, for all the good and perfect things come from Him. He is the fire that lights your way, the compass that shows where to go, He is your hope and lifter of your head. Let Him take Center Stage in your life.

CONCLUSION

Not I but Christ be honored loved exalted
Not I but Christ be seen be known be heard
Not I but Christ in every look and action
Not I but Christ in every thought and word.
(Fanny E. Bolton Hymn 271).

It has been years of toil, research and prayer, but I say with the songwriter, It will be worth it all, when we see Jesus. I give Him praise for using me. Like Moses, I was no match for the task, but the Lord through the Holy Spirit, helped me.

Dear Reader, it is now your turn to heed the call. Center Stage has been through many trying times to get to this point, and it is not meant to offend anyone. For those who are experiencing this exposure for the first time just take courage from the end of the life of Nebuchadnezzar. He repented and God saved him. If you are like the prodigal son, the Father is waiting to welcome you home. If you are like the Samaritan woman at the well, Jesus is passing your way today to offer you living water so you will never thirst again. If you are experiencing challenges from others, remember Daniel, Joseph and Moses, their end was more glorious than they could imagine. If your experiences differ in any way, God can fix any situation. Satan will fight and discourage you, but remember earth has no sorrow that heaven cannot heal.

The enemy has put up many gallant fights, to discourage me from writing this book, but every time he rushed in, Michael defeated him. One such major attempt was the disappearance of the first manuscript after almost its completion (still missing even as I write). Disappointment was a mild feeling. After a year of struggle and coming to grips with the reality, "start over," was what I was told. This is it my friends. This is for you. Do not procrastinate, do it now. May the God of peace keep you and give you the courage to accept Jesus who is waiting for you to come to Him. There is no middle ground, there is no way around the truth, and the Bible has spoken. What will it be, man's opinion and tradition, or thus says the Lord?

My friends, heaven is waiting for you to say yes to the invitation Jesus gives you. Come to Him, just as you are today. Hear His voice today harden not your heart. The Savior is waiting to enter your heart. Accept Him now so His blood can cover your sin and set you free. There is nothing in the world that is worth exchanging for your salvation. "The friendship of Jesus is . . . the pearl of great price." (Andros, 2006). Jesus said, "Ye are my friends, if ye do whatsoever I command you."

Remember, Jesus is doing His closing work of judgment in the heavenly Sanctuary, and He is coming with His reward. The signs of the time tell us His time to complete the judgment is almost finished. When He pronounces, "It is finished," that will be it. There will be no more repentance for sin. Do it now. He loves you and wants to save you. He does not want anyone to perish. He wants to save you now. He wants to occupy the Center Stage of your life. May the God of peace give you the courage to accept Him today.

Appendix A

Charlemagne

King of the Franks and Lombards

Some of his accomplishments include:

Introducing the jury system, turning his castle into a learning center, and invited scholars to make illuminated manuscripts thus preserving knowledge in the dark ages.

Defeating the barbarian tribes in Western Europe

Expanding the Frankish Empire to include Germany, France, sections of North Spain and most of Italy.

He helped Pope Leo111 squash a rebellion and was crowned Emperor of Rome, December 25, 800. This event marked the beginning of the Holy Roman Empire and paved the way for the Empire to become the dominant religion of the Christian sects.

He also engaged in horrific crimes:

Moral indecency and depravity for the purpose of extortion.

Moral indecency and depravity for the purpose of coordinating satanic human sacrifice. He murdered Saxon priests who did not convert or pay tribute to the Roman Catholic Church

He ordered the unlawful murder of 4500 Saxon prisoners of war at Verden.

Charlemagne
From "The Dark Ages" documentary
www.lucidcafe.com

APPENDIX B

Modifying the Law

"It [the Roman Catholic Church] reversed the Fourth Commandment by doing away with the Sabbath of God's word, and instituting Sunday as holyday."
N. Summerbell, *History* of the Christian Church (1873), p. 415.

God gave the Sabbath to man so he would keep Him in mind as Creator . . ." it can be readily seen that a power endeavoring to exalt itself above God could do this in no other way so effectually as by setting aside God's memorial-the seventh-day Sabbath." A woe is pronounced on those who add or change God's command. Man needs to obey the 'Thus saith the Lord.' "To this work of the Papacy, Daniel had reference when he said, "And he shall . . . think to change times and laws."

James Cardinal Gibbons says, "You may read the Bible from Genesis to Revelation, and you will not see a single line authorizing the sanctification of Sunday. The Scriptures enforce the observance of Saturday, a day which we never sanctify."—James Cardinal Gibbons—The *Faith of Our Fathers* (1917 ed.), pp. 72, 73,

(*Bible Reading for the Home* pp. 193, 194)

See other references:

Catechism of the Council of Trent (Donovan translation 1867). Part 3 chap 4, p. 345).

Henry Tuberville, An *Abridgement of the Christian Doctrine* (1883 approbation) p.58

Stephen Keenan, *A Doctrinal Catechism* (3rd ed.), p. 174.

The Catholic Mirror, official organ of Cardinal Gibbons, Sept, 23, 1893.

Appendix C

The Beast and the Law of God.

Revelation 13 speaks to the beast, the mark of the beast, and image. It shows that the two-horned beast erects the image and enforces the law. The "beast" is the Roman Catholic power.

The "mark of the beast" is the institution set forth by this power to legislate for the church, and change the law of God, taking the away God's signature of royalty from the law.

The seventh-day Sabbath, the great memorial of creation, is chiseled out of the Decalogue, and replaced by a false sabbath, the first day of the week.

The "image of the beast" an ecclesiastical power, resembling the beast clothed with power to it laws with the penalties of civil law.

The "two-horned beast" the United States of America, enforces the mark of the beast that is, establishing by law the observance of the first day of the week, as the rest day.

Revelation 14:6-12 warn against false worship. Verse 9, exposes the work of the beast, and warns the people against compliance with its demands.

There is a movement that has made proclaiming the truth of God and warning against reception of policies of the beast. It has shown that the mark of the beast is dressed in Christian garb and is introduced in Christian Churches in a subtle way to nullify the authority of Jehovah, and introduce the authority of the beast

Verse 12, proves the correctness of the position of the movement. "Here is the patience of the saints: here are they that keep the commandments of God, and the faith of Jesus
(Daniel and the Revelation pp. 618-621).

APPENDIX D

The Hussites

The Hussites were orthodox Christians who were followers of John Huss. He was declared a heretic and he died at the stake in 1418. John thought the lay people had the ability to understand the Bible by themselves so he encouraged them to read the scriptures. He had some concerns, which included:

- Immorality of the priesthood
- Financial abuses
- Sexual immorality
- Desire to include all Christian in full communion
- The selling of indulgences

However, his main concern was that the Bible and Scriptures should be placed first in importance over the Church leaders and councils. The people should depend on the Bible for their religion, not the leaders.

He was arrested, imprisoned, and compelled to retract his statement and obey the church completely. He refused to recant, but rather sang praises to God even when the fire was consuming him. After his death, the remaining Hussites, some went underground others left their homeland or settled with the church. Huss' influence did not only affect those who followed him, but had great impact on the Protestant Reformation.

http://myweb.tiscall.co.uk/matthaywood/main/Hussites.htm

APPENDIX E

The Little Horn

The papacy had reached a time in prophecy, in A. D. 538, where it would dominate over the minds of men. The little horn forcibly plucked out three horns from the ten horns. Daniel 7:20, says that the three horns were overcome by it. These horns were the kingdoms of Heruli, Vandals, and Ostrogoths, who were also called barbarians.

Odoacer was the first leader of Heruli to rule over the Romans and took the throne of Italy in A.D. 476. He honored the monastic and Episcopal characters, and there was a level of tolerance among them and the Catholics. On the other hand, the Ostrogoths and Vandals liked the simple lessons of the common teachers, so they adopted the teachings. Arianism became their national faith. The Arian doctrine had a great impact on the then church, but after a while, the church fell and pagan people took the rule of Britain. The Arian kings and Lombards took portions and set up their kingdom in close proximity to the gates of Rome.

The Roman bishops surrounded on every side exerted themselves with prudence to regain control at least over their patriarchal diocese. However, the emperors and nations were opposed to the yoke placed on the people by the see of Rome. The Gothic princes set bounds to the control the power of the bishop of Rome, so much so that when Pope Simplicius died in A. D. 483, and the clergy and people met to elect new pope, Odoacer declared their actions null and void, for the simple reason that he was not present. Zeno emperor of the East gave Theodore of the Astrogothic kingdom in Mœsia and Pannonia permission to attack Odoacer and take Italy. After a five-year war, the Herulian kingdom of Italy was overthrown and Odoacer was killed.

Theodoric an Arian summoned Pope John into his presence for persecuting the Arians in **A.D. 523**. He ordered him to go to Constantinople and argue for the restoration and religious freedom for the Arians who were driven away. He was not to set foot on Italian soil until his orders were carried out.

Not only were the Catholics under restrain in Italy, but those in Africa were persecuted by the Arian Vandals. Such was the situation that in A.D. 533, Justinian started the Vandals and Gothic wars. In order to gain favor from the pope and Catholic party, he decreed that the pope was the head of all the churches. **Thus A.D. 538, marked the year of papal supremacy**. The Catholics consider Belisarius, the general of Justinian.

Thus, the three horns were plucked up by the little horn:

The Heruli, A.D. 493
The Vandals A.D. 534
The Ostrogoths A.D. 553

Daniel and the Revelation pp. 107-113

APPENDIX F

The 1260 Days Period

This forty-two months or 1260 prophetic year prophecy, started in A.D. 538, And ended in A. D. 1798. This marked the end of Rome's rule. This fulfills the prediction of the wounding of the beast. Revelation 12:6, the woman which is the church, fled into the wilderness for a period of 1260 days (1260) years. This period was known as the dark ages when the church of God went underground, because of persecution from Rome. Verse 14 speaks of the woman fleeing into the wilderness and being nourished for three and a half years (which is equivalent to forty-two months), from the face of the serpent.

The time period mentioned in Both Daniel and Revelation, is clarified thus, time represents 12 months,(which is '12' 30-day months) hence "times" would be 2 twelve month periods which would total 24 months or 2 years, and ½ "time" would be half of 360 which is 180. Hence "time" = 30× 12 =360, "times"=30 x 24 =720, then 360+180+720=1260 or in months it would be "time and "times= 3 years and ½ a "time" = six months = (3x12) +6 =42 months.

"A prophetic year means 360 prophetic days, but a prophetic day stands for a solar year." [1]

A Jewish calendar year, which could be a lunar of variable length and a solar calendar year of 365 days, should not be confused with the prophetic year of 360 days. [2]

The church suffered a great papal apostasy during this period, and they were oppressed and scattered. However, a great blessing resulted from this scattering of the Christians, because they took the gospel of truth where they went. God was about to use a remnant to scatter seeds of the truth, so during the Reformation of the 16ᵗʰ century He led various Protestant groups to restore the glorious gospel of truth. Many of these groups however, were satisfied with partial truth and were not willing to advance, as the light from God's word increased. As groups fail to advance, God would raise up new ones to proclaim the truth.

The final remnant was raised up at the close of the 1260 years; this remnant is designated in *Revelation* 12:17. This is God's last day herald appointed to preach the final appeal to the world to accept the gracious gift of salvation. (*Revelation* 14:6-12). Seventh Day Adventist humbly believe that they are the remnant that is now proclaiming the messages of *Revelation* 14—calling sinners to accept Christ, and meets the specification of *Revelation* 12: 17.

However, Seventh Day Adventist do not believe nor teach that they have any claim on heaven, nor think that they alone are the children of God. "They believe that all who worship God in full sincerity, that is, in terms of all the revealed will of God that they understand, are presently potential members of that final "remnant" company mentioned in Revelation 12: 17."[3]

[1 & 2] S.D.A. Bible Commentary Bk. 4 p. 833

[3]   S.D.A. Bible Commentary Bk. 7 p. 815

Appendix G

A.D. 457-B.C. 1844

"Why *in 1844?* The query may here arise how the days can be extended to the **autumn of 1844** if they begin in **457 B.C.,** as it requires only 1843 years, in addition to the **457,** to make 2300 years. One fact will "hopefully" clear this point of all difficulties. It takes 457 full years before Christ, and 1843, full years after to make 2300 years. There are no zero years, so **457 B.C.** to **456 B.C.** is one year, in the same way, 1843-1844, is one year. (In B.C. we subtract years) Example, a child born in July 2010, would celebrate his birthday in July 2011. Even though there are two years involved the reckoning would be the same twelve months, July 2010 to July 2011 is one year, and cannot be calculated as two years, since there are no zero years. Now it will be evident to all that if any of the year of 457 had passed away before the 2300 days began, just so much of the year 1844 must pass away before the fulfillment would end.

The decree was given in **457 B.C.** but went into effect autumn of that year, which was actually seven months into **457 B.C.,** (the point from which the decree would be reckoned). The **forty-nine** years were allotted to the building of the street and wall. The next sixty-two weeks, or (434 years) would see the completion of the work already started down to the baptism and anointing of Jesus. The period is to be dated, not from the actual beginning of the work in Jerusalem. This beginning could hardly be earlier than the seventh month (autumn) of 457, as he did not arrive at Jerusalem until the **fifth** month of that year, and the work started two months later. (*Ezra* 7: 9.) The whole period would therefore extend to the seventh month, autumn, Jewish time 1844. (*Daniel & the Revelation* p. 200). It is reasonable to deduce that since the decree began Autumn of **457 B.C.** this beginning period is closer to **456 B.C.**

APPENDIX H

The "Daily"

Daniel 8:11 says, the daily sacrifice was taken away. Papal Rome assumed the role of priest and intercessor, and caused craft and deceit to succeed.

The other replied in verse 14, "Unto two thousand three hundred days; then shall the sanctuary be cleansed."

In chapter 17, the little horn blasphemed against the most High, and persecuted the saints. This little horn is Rome in its pagan and Papal forms that tread upon the commands or ministry of Christ and His saints.

Magnified himself:

- Removes God's laws
- Changes times and laws, the Sabbath
- Claims duties of God

The sanctuary, of which the verse speaks, maqdash, depicts an evil sanctuary. (See *Isaiah* 62:12, *Ezekiel* 28:18). Daniel defines clearly the difference between this sanctuary and the sanctuary found in verse 13. The Pantheon Rome's place of worship and Rome itself lost fame when Constantine moved the seat of Rome to Constantinople in the East in 330 A.D. The seat of Rome and the Pantheon faded in significance as papal

Rome adopted pagan idols, traditions, superstitious rites, and idolatrous ceremonies. (see on *Revelation* 13:2).

Clovis king of the Franks and many others defended the papacy. He was converted to Catholicism in 496 A.D. In turn, he converted other pagan nations of Western Europe through war and capitulations. In 1996, Pope John Paul 11 went to France to celebrate the centenary of the baptism of Clovis, pagan leader and first Western Christian king and founder of the modern French nation. The combining of church and state is deemed the transgression or the breaking of the law.

www.teachinghearts .org/drc17

BIBLE SYMBOLS

Symbols	Meanings	References
Angels Flying	Speed	Revelation 14:6-12
Babylon (Ancient)	Symbol of opposition against Christ and His followers	Daniel 1:1, Jer. 51:9, Rev. 14:7, 17:8
Babylon (Modern)	Divided kingdoms of Rome	Isa. 21:9, Daniel 2, Sam. 17:8, Prov. 17:12, Hosea 5:9
Bear	Represents Medo-Persia in the image of Nebuchadnezzar	Daniel 2, 2 Sam. 17:8, Prov. 17:12, Hosea 13:8, Amos 5:19
Beast	Symbol of World Power in conflict with God's people	Rev. 13:2, Dan. 7:23
Brass (Bronze)	Kingdom of Greece (Belly and thigh of the image)	Daniel 2:32
Daily	Divinely ordained system of worship	Daniel 8:11-13, 11:31, 12:11
Day (1)	Hebrews calendar day (sunset to sunset)	Lev. 22:6&7, Mark 1:32
Day (2)	In the New Testament a day is from sunrise to sunset	Matt. 20:1-12, John 11:9
Day (3)	One Prophetic day, one literal year	Ezek. 4:6, Num. 14:34
Dragon	Enmity against God and His chosen people, also represents Satan.	Ezek. 29:3-5, 32:2-8, Isa. 27:1, 51:9, Psalm 74:13, Rev. 12

206

Fornication	Spiritual apostasy	Rev. 17:2, 29:2
Gold	Symbolizes great value and worth	Prov. 25:12, Lam. 4:2, Rev 3:18
He –Goat	In the symbolic dream of Daniel, the he-goat represents the Hellenistic empire of Alexander.	Daniel 8:5 & 21
Host (1)	Armies of the Lord of Host	1 Sam. 1:3 & 11, 1 Kings 18:15, James 5:4, Rom. 9:29
Host (2)	Celestial bodies worshipped by heathen nations	Dan. 8, Jer. 8:2, 19:13, Zeph. 1:5, Acts 7:42, Rev. 12:3-6
Horns	Kings, kingdoms, other powers, arrogance	Dan. 7:8, 20-21 & 24, Rev. 17:12 &16
Image of the Beast	Symbolizes the worship of false gods in various forms and the worship of images	Rev. 14:11-15
Lamb	Jesus the Lamb of God	Rev 8:8,14 & 19:6,7
Leopard	Symbol of world power (Greece)	Jer. 4:7, 50:17,43,44, Dan. 7:6, Rev. 13:2
Lion	Represents Babylon, symbol of strength and courage, whether divine or human.	Gen. 49:9, Job 100:16, Dan 2:41, 8:24, 25. Hos. 5:14, 11:10, 13:7, Jer. 25:38, Rev 5:5, Dan 2:41, 8:24,25
Little horn	Symbol for a great foe of God's people	Dan. 7:8, 20-26, 8:9-14, 23-26
Ram (1)	In prophecy, the ram is a symbol of Persia	Dan 8:3,20
Ram (2)	In Hebrew, the term is a symbol for a leader or a mighty man.	Ex. 15:15, Ezek. 17:13
Time and Time	Symbolic prophecy of 360 days for a year	Ezek. 4:6, Num. 14:34
	31/2 days then is equal to 31/2 years of 360 days in the year 3yrs *360=1080 years ½yrs*360=180 years =1260 years	Dan 7:25, 11:13, Heb. 12:7, Rev. 12:14

Waters	Symbolize peoples, nations, multitudes and tongues	Rev 17:15
Wings	Symbol of speed, angels of Revelation	Rev 14:6-12
	Alexander the great/Greece	Hab. 1:6-8
Woman	Symbolizes the church: -pure woman pure church -impure woman (Babylon) impure church	Rev 17:1-6,18
Wounded	Beast dethroned in 1798	Rev 13:3

References:

Anderson, M., Caviness, L. L., Chrestensen, O. H., Cottrell, R. F., Froom, L. E., Hammill, R., Harding, L. . . . Yost, F., H. (1980), SDA Bible Commentary, Review and Herald Publishing Association, Haggertown, MD.

Andros, M. E. (2006), Alone with God Pacific Press, Nampa, Idaho.

ASI Missions (1990), Bible Reading Better Living Publications

Charlemagne Retrieved from www.charlemagne.com www.lucidcafe.com

Daniel Bible Prophecy, The Ram and the Goat Daniel 8, Retrieved from: www.teachingheart.org

Goodsalt Images, Retrieved from: www.goodsalt.com

Retzer, F., and Speegle, M.(1996),You can Understand the Bible, Review and Herald Publishing Association, Haggertowm MD.

Smith, U., (1944), Daniel and the Revelation/Treasures of Life, Pacific Press Mountain View California.

The Bohemia Hussites, Retrieved from http://myweb.trscan.co/uk/matthayhood/main/Hussites.htm

The Great Controversy Ended . . . (1990) Better Living Publications

White, E. G., (1908), Steps to Christ Review and Herald Publishing Association Haggertown MD.

ABOUT THE AUTHOR

Norma P. Gillett, Dip., Cert., B.A., M.A.,in Education, is an Educator and Church Elder in South Florida, U.S.A.,past principal of Roehampton Primary School, and past elder of Anchovy S.D.A. Church, Saint James Jamaica. She loves the Lord and is passionate about being a witness of His love. She thinks falling in love with Jesus is the best thing she has ever done.